Management by Inspiration

Discovering Your Natural
Power to Lead

by

Allan E. Flood, MS

CCB Publishing
British Columbia, Canada

Management by Inspiration: Discovering Your Natural Power to Lead

Copyright ©1991, 2020 by Allan E. Flood
ISBN-13 978-1-77143-423-2
Second Edition

Library and Archives Canada Cataloguing in Publication
Title: Inspiration : discovering your natural power to lead / by Allan E. Flood, MS.
Other titles: Management by inspiration
Names: Flood, Allan E., author.
Description: Second edition. | First edition published under title:
Management by inspiration | Includes bibliographical references.
Identifiers: Canadiana (print) 20200265199 | Canadiana (ebook) 20200265296
| ISBN 9781771434232 (softcover) | ISBN 9781771434249 (PDF)
Subjects: LCSH: Management. | LCSH: Leadership.
Classification: LCC HD31 .F567 2020 | DDC 658—dc23

Cover design by Debra Rudloff.

Allan E. Flood contact information:
Facebook: https://www.facebook.com/allan000000
Facebook: https://www.facebook.com/allan.flood.18
E-mail: aflood@q.com

Publisher: CCB Publishing
                British Columbia, Canada
                www.ccbpublishing.com

Dedication

To Buster:
I understand better now.

Table of Contents

Are there secrets to managing human relations? Is there anything that makes it easier, more natural and more enjoyable to motivate and work with other people?

How can I gauge whether my employees and I are really using our wisdom to make decisions and solve problems?

Acknowledgments

This book is a blend of heart and mind. I'd like to express my thanks to the many people who have previewed drafts and provided their honest appraisals. I'd especially like to thank Dr. Rita Shuford and Sandra Krot of The Florida Center for Human Development in Tampa, Florida, for their encouragement; Bonnie Barrett for the many insightful and rewarding lunches we spent discussing these pages and the principles within them; Caroline Hall Otis who, as editor, brought clarity to the manuscript; and Mike and Linda Corcoran, who have applied the principles to their business and are reaping the benefits. Finally, I'd like to thank Nancy for being the litmus test for everything I've learned.

I'd also like to thank the many others at The Florida Center for Human Development whose conversations, tapes and books have helped me preserve my common sense.

I'd like to express my deepest gratitude for the writings and inspiration of Sydney Banks. More than forty years ago he showed me a less complicated way to approach life.

Introduction

On the wall of my den, there's a framed black and white photograph of myself as a young boy. Wearing a striped T-shirt, I am looking into the camera. My father took it when I was four or five years old. I keep it displayed because my face has a very special quality that I can only describe as profound tranquility. For the longest time, I thought I'd lost the feeling behind that look.

I remember, as a child, enthusiastically saving bugs trapped in swimming pools, staring into the wonder of ocean tide pools and exploring the woods behind our house. I'm beginning to recapture those feelings of fascination and involvement, of caring for the great outdoors and of living from inspiration rather than plan. Happily, as my understanding of the facts presented in this book deepens, these feelings have become a fundamental part of my business and personal relationships.

In that old black and white picture I'm quietly looking at the picture-taker, not distracted by a multitude of fears, beliefs and judgments. It's the direct, powerful look of someone at peace. Business leaders who live in this state of mind appreciate its practical value and use their wisdom to promote work environments free of the flotsam and jetsam of the human thought process. They create organizations with genuinely inspired employees. Performance born of inspiration and wisdom leads to excellence. When it's driven by fear and anxiety, however, it leads to pain, stress, burnout and, ultimately, low achievement.

This book is dedicated to those fortunate people who work with and manage others. The approach to life I describe in these pages will help you get the best out of your employees and colleagues. It's a breath of fresh air for managers who are tired of fighting personnel fires and who seek a different way to lead people.

I wrote this book to explain what you must have, *beyond information,* to lead effectively. Managers need more than new variations of old approaches. In this age of escalating complexity, business leaders need a fresh understanding of the underlying forces that motivate people.

You've already tried incentives and methods to increase performance. Some worked, some didn't—most worked only temporarily. However, the success of whatever you use depends on simple, profound facts. It's been said that an idea whose time has come is stronger than all the armies in the world. The simple facts presented here are ideas whose time has come, *fundamental insights* about the way human beings function.

The truths in this book help you manage in the same way that a clear business vision helps you make decisions. A clear business vision simplifies problem-solving because it provides context and direction. When you know where your vision comes from and how to maintain it, you're like the sailboat captain who can keep his or her ship on course despite changes in wind, weather and currents.

As you see how the simple truths in this book affect you, your management style will reflect a deeper, practical knowledge of how to vitalize your business and your employees. My own journey, which began with realizing the extraordinary power of these simple truths, has been one of amazement and wonder at innate human potential. After years of following the ebb and flow of popular fads in management and mental health, I've found something truly enduring.

So feed the cat, stoke the fire, pour yourself a steaming hot cup of coffee and start turning the pages. I think you're going to enjoy this new adventure.

Management
by
Inspiration

Discovering Your Natural
Power to Lead

Chapter 1

Management Secrets

Are there secrets to managing human relations? Is there anything that makes it easier, more natural and more enjoyable to motivate and work with other people?

The answer is yes. There *are* keys to managing people effectively. The quality of the techniques we employ is important, yes. But, as I'll show in this book, what's really *vital* to productive leadership is *the depth of our self-understanding.*

Employee motivating techniques abound. We can nurture creativity and enthusiasm via profit-sharing programs and hundreds of other methods designed to boost performance so that everybody wins. There is also a myriad of how-to books on influencing employee performance. If the key to effective leadership lay solely in gathering and applying information we'd be in great shape. There is plenty at hand. In fact, there's more information available than the interested manager could digest in a lifetime. But, so far, it hasn't really done the job. The final answer to effective management lies somewhere *outside* the techniques we use.

Techniques: A Time and A Place

Take a look at these popular techniques for increasing productivity in the workplace:

- Tie compensation to performance
- Pay salespeople more than executives
- Hold yearly award dinners
- Scrap job descriptions for performance appraisals
- Make wage and salary decisions public
- Give holiday bonuses
- Involve employees in every decision
- Continually train and retrain
- Be generous with base pay
- Sponsor company golf tournaments
- Share ownership with employees

Using techniques as a way to change behavior is a carrot-and-stick approach to improving performance. The assumption here is that managing people is like riding a donkey. You need carrots (positive incentives) to keep the donkey interested, and sticks (disciplinary actions) to keep the beast moving when his interest wanes. The problem is that you continually have to increase the number of carrots and the size of the stick to get results.

Techniques increase motivation and productivity, at least temporarily, but even successful methods can lose their effectiveness over time. Profit-sharing boosts performance as long as it's tied to factors employees can control. Bonuses are taken for granted, award ceremonies become a nuisance, and employees tire of being involved in every decision. Sometimes the donkey won't walk no matter how many carrots you give it or how big the stick is. Carrot-and-stick management can also create administrative complexity. Complicated profit-sharing plans and lists of regulations are examples of details created by this approach. When we use techniques without understanding the intrinsic forces that make them work, we benefit in the same way that vacationing regenerates us temporarily. Using techniques without self-understanding is like taking Valium for ongoing stress; it treats the symptoms rather than the cause.

Business leaders who fail to increase motivation via techniques usually discover that there's a crucial dimension missing. This other aspect of performance has to do with how well managers and employees understand the _source_ and _nature_ of their attitudes. In fact, using techniques successfully over the long haul depends on understanding certain basic facts about how the mind works.

What follows are some examples of techniques applied without understanding. A business colleague of mine tried to implement quality circles in a large wood products company. However the process fell through at the eleventh hour when it became apparent that there wasn't enough trust between the union and management. Quality circles, under these circumstances, could never be anything but a token venture. Techniques don't work when they require exceeding existing levels of understanding between parties. And, when management isn't ready to share power and control with employees, methods for increasing productivity don't work well or for long. For years, our manufacturing company had an annual golf tournament attended by everybody (whether they golfed or not). One Christmas (we played in December because we were in Southern California) it became clear that nobody cared about it anymore except for a few executives and employees who enjoyed playing golf. Most employees avoided the event if they could. It had lost its motivating power because the positive feelings that had created it had disappeared.

We also tried using timeclocks (stick techniques) to ensure accountability. We required our employees to come to work very early during the summer, sometimes at 4:00 or 5:00 a.m., because Southern California afternoons were so hot. When they objected, we installed time clocks to ensure their prompt arrival. After a few months, however, we discovered that certain employees were punching in early for everybody else. Using techniques to force behaviors from unwilling people usually backfires.

My grandfather, the president of a large paper mill, created resentment by sending his executives on lavish vacations and then asking them to make sales calls during their trips. He genuinely believed he was doing them a favor. Because his understanding was limited, however, he misused the technique (a free, no-strings attached vacation) and created ill will.

In the early 1980's, human relationship specialists focused on communication training, which teaches you how to tell other people clearly what you want while taking responsibility for your feelings. Participants quickly discovered that communication tricks like "I" statements ("I feel angry when you do such and such.") designed to encourage personal responsibility, were easily abused depending on the speaker's mood. When we're feeling negative, our judgments sneak effortlessly past the techniques we apply to sound nonjudgmental. The neutral statement, "I feel angry when you slam the door," can easily come across as, "You really tick me off when you slam the door. If you do it again, you're in deep trouble, pal!" Just as management's attitude is more important than techniques to ensure long-term productivity, effective communication depends more on the communicator's attitude than the communication's structure and content.

The message is clear: Solving management problems requires something more than techniques. What, then, does management need to know to elicit long-term, consistent high performance and motivation?

Understanding: The Foundation

The key to successful application of human relations management techniques is our *understanding*.

Understanding is both the process and result of learning certain profound facts of mental functioning. Self-understanding includes perceiving the pitfalls of thinking, the role feelings play in our lives, and how remarkable our creative abilities actually are.

Understanding means seeing how our thinking and emotions affect our perceptions and actions. Self-understanding—internalizing those truths—is where it all begins. Self-understanding *always* yields the wisdom to solve human relations problems. It enables us to trust and respect our employees and co-workers which, in turn leads to their high motivation and productivity.

Understanding: A Story

The following story illustrates the potency of self-understanding in resolving a difficult situation. It shows how Linda and her husband Mike, the owners of a growing high-tech manufacturing company, began to use the power of understanding in their workplace. Prior to the incident described here, I shared the concept of self-understanding with the company's management and staff. Linda told me this story about a salesman I'll call John.

"We hired John three months ago to sell our product. He was a former copier salesman who had a personality like Herb on *WKRP in Cincinnati*—caricature of a huckster with a negative attitude. John had had dozens of jobs and we weren't at all sure he'd work out.

"Two weeks ago John started pressing for a raise of $250 a month. He said Mike, my husband, had promised him the raise after three months of work. Mike was certain, however, he had done no such thing. The raise would put John well above what anyone has ever earned at our company.

"John was unhappy with our philosophy that everyone was important to the team. He told another employee that sales personnel are the most important people in a company and should be treated as such. He also felt he should get a larger share of profit than anyone else.

"Considering our differences, it's amazing we worked together for three months. John constantly complained about personal problems and was the only one who didn't like our new incentive plan's evaluation system.

"After a few months, Mike and I sat down with John and outlined what he was doing well and what we'd like him to do differently. He countered every point with an excuse. He disagreed ("I'm already doing that.") and argued that we didn't need whatever we asked him to do. He left our meeting disgruntled, saying he would have to think about working for us. He stayed home the next day.

"In the meantime, I made up my mind to get rid of John because he was *so* stubborn. He absolutely refused to consider any of our suggestions. He seemed completely out of tune with our company goals. Also, other employees encouraged us to fire him since he wasn't pulling his share of the load.

"Yesterday morning John told us that, although he wants more money, he'd decided to stay because he believes in the company. I said we needed to agree about what was expected of him. Instantly, we fell back into the old pattern of me suggesting, him defending, me getting angry and him getting angry. I just *couldn't* believe he really wanted to work for us. He finally shouted that we were being unfair and we needed to decide whether or not to keep him.

"John went back to his office. Mike and I agreed there was little choice but to fire him. We started discussing how much severance pay to provide.

"Mike left to take a phone call and I began to work on a computer program. I thought about John, sitting in his office, waiting for us to decide his fate. I became aware of a large ball of sadness in my heart. My head told me not to feel sorry for John when I should be thinking about the good of the company, but my sad feeling was *so* intense.

"When my husband returned, I explained my feelings. I told him we had a communication problem with John. We asked John to rejoin us and I shared how I felt about our miscommunications. I was so overwhelmed, I had trouble speaking.

"Because of what I'd learned about self-understanding, I knew that my perception of the world, not the world itself, was probably wrong. With that realization, my feelings changed from blame and defensiveness to curiosity. I wondered about my sadness and my problems with John.

"I saw that I sometimes blame other people for negative things that happen to me. This time, however, instead of blaming John, I saw my own part in creating my sad feelings. And then I saw John's innocence—how he was being driven through life by fear and a lack of understanding. He simply didn't see how he was creating his own emotional pain. My heart went out to him.

"As we talked, the ball of sadness changed into a ball of love the size of a basketball. I felt I had a new organ for perceiving people's vulnerability and softness. This feeling persisted throughout the day.

"Because I saw the situation more clearly, John, Mike and I dealt with the important issues more easily. We talked about trust and discussed what we could do to rebuild it. John admitted he always runs from problems and that's why he likes to go on the road. We explained how that behavior makes us feel—he travels to escape rather than for the good of our business. He understood.

"John went back to work and put in more obvious effort than ever before. He even went to the library and checked out books we asked him to read.

"While I'm pleased about John's new attitude, I want to stress my own change. I've experienced what really feels like a miracle. All my long-standing anger towards John has turned into feelings of love and appreciation. How incredible. One minute I was one person and the next I was a different one with a new perspective. My jump in self-understanding literally took care of the problem.

"Looking back at our employee problems, I see that they're all similar and, therefore, easier to solve. I'm also struck by how *fast* we can solve our problems. Resolution doesn't take any period of growth or complex techniques. Within the next few weeks, I believe that all of us will finally be able to focus on business rather than get bogged down in relationship problems."

Linda had run out of ideas for working with John. Anyway, no technique would have been effective, given John's negative attitude. What Linda needed was *new* information, information available only through a jump in self-understanding.

The positive feeling that comes from self-understanding leads directly to understanding others. Self-understanding heals personal rifts, resolves doubts and cures confusion. When Linda experienced the transformation from sadness to compassion and appreciation and her understanding rose, she communicated better, listened more effectively, and saw the problem and what needed to be done more clearly. Her positive feelings boosted her ability to solve problems and make decisions. In this understanding environment, John also communicated better and listened rather than reacting defensively. Because both parties could see the problem clearly, free of conflict and confusion, the solutions surfaced much more easily.

The understanding I describe in these pages and that Linda felt goes beyond the dictionary definition of "being sympathetically disposed." Instead, it means grasping the significance of how the mind works (such as when Linda suddenly *understood* in her heart and mind that the source of John's behavior was insecurity).

When a manager gains understanding, the results are sometimes subtle and sometimes dramatic, but they're always positive and open new doors of possibilities. Understanding—starting with self-understanding—is the beginning of inspired management. A business that operates with understanding is free to expand in ways it can't even imagine.

Understanding works in a business just like intimacy works in a relationship. When two people lose their feeling of intimacy, it doesn't matter what they do together; everything is less enjoyable. When they have intimacy, however, virtually everything they do is pleasurable. The *long-term* cure for a "no fun" relationship is recapturing feelings of intimacy, not in going to new places and trying new things—both technique solutions.

When understanding is absent in business—usually manifested as a lack of vision—problems are overwhelming. Managers in this climate find themselves running in place. Again, solutions are not to be found in trying new things. Creating organizational enthusiasm isn't like directing a cruise ship social program—people don't have to be entertained to stay motivated. Trying lots of new activities in order to solve problems might be called "technique frenzy." And technique frenzy doesn't work.

My definition of understanding includes appreciating the pitfalls of the thinking process, the central role feelings play in our lives and how remarkable our abilities and potential for creativity actually are. Business leaders who realize what self-understanding is, where it comes from, and how to nurture and promote it in the work environment create organizations where people naturally cooperate, work hard and use common sense to make decisions and solve problems.

As children, many of us had the opportunity to work with two bosses who treated us with compassion born of self-understanding. Although parents can be impatient, authoritarian and stubborn, at their best they are firm, loving, supportive and even wise. During those good times, children are also at their best.

I remember my first experience with alcohol. I drank way too much, certain it wouldn't affect me, and paid for it with a terrible two-day hangover. I was in awful physical pain the next day but worse, I was in emotional pain, too. I felt I'd let my parents down and deserved whatever punishment I got. But you know what? They saw the agony I was going through and were compassionate about it—far more so than I thought they would be. Their *understanding* (they had a hunch I'd do something dumb like that eventually and they loved me anyway) overpowered their anger and disappointment. I never forgot their compassion and learned as much about families, relationships, parenting and love as I did about vodka that day.

The same understanding that makes for good parents makes for successful business leaders. People who manage with compassion command loyalty, respect, performance and motivation.

During summer vacations while I was in college, I worked as a stock boy for a paint store. My supervisor was a crusty, tattooed man named Ed. He'd been in the paint business forever. When I first started working there, I dreaded dealing with Ed because we disagreed about values, the way we dressed and politics. Nevertheless, Ed turned out to be a great boss. He had high expectations for all his employees and treated each of us with trust and respect. He knew that if you respect an employee he or she will work hard for you and the company. And I did. I was on time, tried my best, valued his praise and listened carefully to his criticism. I appreciated working there despite the job's low prestige and pay, and I have fond memories of the paint store—and of Ed.

Self-understanding creates positive feelings—the feelings we have when we're functioning well as human beings. Our thoughts serve us rather than trip us up, we're not distracted, judgmental, angry or depressed, and we're not caught in the hurricane of negative emotions. In a nutshell, we're at our best.

A common misconception about understanding leaders is that they're indecisive, weak and unable to discipline. The same understanding that disposes us towards kindness, compassion and tolerance, however, inhibits indecisiveness. When people understand themselves, that deep, powerful feeling gives them the courage and wisdom to make difficult decisions.

Understanding executives, managers and supervisors know where the company is going and how everybody contributes to the journey. They know when they or their employees are interfering with the positive momentum they want. Self-understanding and its result, managerial inspiration, is what this book is about.

It's actually pretty simple. In order to manage others in a way that's easier, more natural and more enjoyable...

- **First, gain self-understanding—or** *personal* **knowledge of certain profound facts about mental functioning, feelings and actions. It is** *the* **foundation of individual and organizational health and prosperity.**

  Self-understanding and the feelings that go along with it (not techniques) are the keys to inspirational management. Your people need self-understanding, too. Groups that work to gether with high levels of this wisdom are motivated and productive.

- **Second, through self-understanding, gain a profound understanding of others.**

  Comprehending others follows naturally as self-understanding increases because we judge less and listen more. We see others' actions and motives clearly, without looking through the filter of our own prejudices and expectations.

- **Third, create a work environment where understanding, common sense and wisdom flourish.**

Creating an organizational climate that supports wisdom and self-understanding is a _fundamental management function_ since it affects the way we make decisions and process information. The policies we set up, our compensation-incentive plans and the way we communicate and delegate authority are opportunities to put self-knowledge and wisdom to work.

Most human relations problems are problems of understanding rather than methodology. When we manage by inspiration, the techniques we choose are a _by-product_ of understanding and positive attitudes. These techniques include guaranteeing salaries, hiring temporaries in boom times to avoid laying off permanent employees in slack periods, tying performance to productivity so employees can control part of their income, giving employees a stake in the company, involving employees in decision-making and problem-solving through participatory management. This list is familiar of course; the arsenal of techniques doesn't change. What makes all the difference in the world is the _attitude_ behind the techniques you choose.

Insecurity is the root of most employee problems. When management-for-performance techniques are backed by understanding, employees feel trusted, respected, secure and in control of their lives. As a result, there is less insecurity around to create problems.

Businesses are made of people working together to achieve goals. Organizations often limp along and even grind to a halt from the friction of human relations conflicts, miscommunications and hostilities that keep people from working together. Understanding is the oil that prevents friction and promotes organizational excellence. Understanding is the foundation of managerial and organizational excellence. The chapters to come explore the profound truths that make up this wisdom—and how they enable us to inspire those we lead.

Chapter 2

Feelings, Moods and Morale:
The Productivity Barometers

How can I gauge whether my employees and I are really using wisdom to make decisions and solve problems?

I was fortunate to be present during the birth of a friend's business over an Italian dinner about a year ago. What a wonderful thing to watch! From the germ of an idea during the salad to the full-fledged business plan by dessert, the process was a joy. When we start a business or relationship, our feelings are positive and our dreams are clear and dynamic. The entity we create out of nothing is alive. When we feel this way, our enthusiasm pushes us past obstacles and the future begins to fill with inspired results.

Sometimes, though, in the day-to-day fighting of battles, our enthusiasm ebbs. We drown in the details of our problems and forget the feelings that brought us to the business or relationship in the first place. Managing and relating by compromise and sacrifice replace managing by inspiration. When understanding and enthusiasm are low, morale falls, people clash and organizational friction grows.

Positive feelings and inspiration are the same side of the coin. When you have one, you have the other and when you lose one, you lose the other. When we forget our dreams, plunge into a dark mood and lose our wisdom and inspiration, it doesn't help to consult experts, strive harder or search the past for causes. *The way back to our original sense of purpose, direction, clarity of thought and enthusiasm is to recover the dream—to recapture the feelings awakened by self-understanding.*

We've all had the experience of rediscovering a dream. It happens periodically in a relationship when, for a few moments, you fall in love all over again. After a hard work day, you discover your spouse asleep on the couch and your heart fills with warmth and caring. I've also seen dreams recovered during business conferences when company owners get together and swap stories. Sometimes, instead of griping, they see their businesses through new eyes. They regain enthusiasm, recapture their vision and return home with a renewed sense of purpose.

The way to keep dreams and the feelings that go along with them alive is to recognize why they fade. Put simply, dreams die in the morass of negative thoughts and emotions. It might be, for example, that our dreams vanish because fear limits our capacity to trust employees and, therefore, our ability to delegate. It might be, for instance, that dreams disappear in the mental anguish of constantly having to prove we're successful. They might, for example, vanish in our frustration with employees who see the world differently than we do. It's all too easy to find "reasons" for the loss of dreams, but the reasons don't really matter. Any problem can be solved if the feelings are there. The truth is, dreams are fueled by positive feelings and killed by negativity. In each of these examples, the way to recover the vision is to notice the underlying forces causing negative thoughts and emotions and recover positive feelings.

Feelings are infallible guides to the value of our thoughts. How many times have you said (or thought) you were sorry, you didn't mean it, you weren't yourself because you were upset? This is an example of self-understanding—the knowledge (in this case, hindsight) that feelings influence the validity of what we think and do. The caliber and accuracy of our thinking rise and fall in direct proportion to the way we feel. The value of our thoughts as a reliable information source diminishes when we're unhappy. On the other hand, positive emotions like contentment, gratitude and compassion are the _source_ of reliable thinking and effective decision-making and problem-solving. Positive feelings allow new information about us, others and the world to flow into our awareness just as open windows let fresh air flow into a room.

For example, I recently spoke to Susan, a client who was upset and angry about an employee. Contrary to what you might think, the problem wasn't with the employee but rather with Susan's low level of understanding. She couldn't make a positive, courageous decision _because her negative feelings were clouding her judgment and perspective._ I provided an environment where she could relax and let her own common sense solve the problem. I knew that as her mood rose, the right solution would surface.

We talked about windsurfing, her vacation and the dreams she had for the company. As we talked about these apparently unrelated issues, she quieted down and started to enjoy herself. When Susan began to describe her vision for her company, she felt better and her wisdom returned. She saw how her employee's behavior affected her business—and her own contribution to the problem—and gained the courage and clarity to act appropriately. Any effort to solve the problem before this point would have been tainted by her upset.

The change from confusion to clarity was *a product of understanding and inspiration,* not effort or plan. Warm emotions were all it took to open the window to the wisdom Susan needed to solve her problems.

We know we're doing our best when we feel satisfied, when our lives are suffused with joy, love and gratitude, and when we're eager and creative. We can tell how we're doing by how we *feel.* That's true of organizations too. Our feelings are absolute barometers of productivity and invaluable tools for evaluating organizational effectiveness. When our employees are enthusiastic, cooperative and creative, we know they're working for the organization's benefit and that the business is producing at peak capacity. Likewise, when we see them resentful, bored or confused, we know the business is not as productive as it could be. We all have different ways of describing what our business looks like when it's effective. One client, the owner of a temporary employment agency, said she wanted her business to be "humming." This strikes me as a good way to describe a finely tuned, effective organization carrying out its mission.

Business leaders are often uncomfortable dealing with feelings—their own and their employees'. I'm no exception. Early on, my engineering and mathematics background led me to believe in "pure logic." The motivational theories I learned then were academic; they had little bearing on the daily operation of the concrete plant where I later worked. A manager's life there consisted mostly of pumping employees up, threatening them, kidding around, nagging them to do better, etc. Theory was irrelevant. I dearly wanted something more real to understand employee performance.

Later, I began to see that *the effect of feelings on productivity* is *pure logic.* It works like this: we're all highly productive when we are satisfied, enthusiastic and enjoy mutual respect and trust. High performance *follows* positive feelings as surely as day follows night. It's as simple as that.

Business leaders must deal with many questions: How do I keep my employees motivated? What incentive programs should I use? How do I deal with absenteeism and drug abuse? The answer is always the same: by promoting positive feelings—satisfaction, enthusiasm, trust and respect—in the workplace.

It doesn't take generous compensation to motivate people, either. I was a VISTA volunteer in Seattle for three years. Volunteers in Service to America is the domestic version of the Peace Corps. Supervised by a sponsoring agency, we were charged with finding ways to "help communities help themselves." Along with several other VISTA volunteers, I planned, developed and staffed projects including a halfway house for ex-mental patients and a 24-hour crisis center. VISTA paid us a whopping $250 a month and the working conditions were marginal. We worked long hours (we were technically on call 24 hours a day) under sometimes stressful conditions (we dealt with suicide attempts, psychotics and angry, violent people). Nevertheless, we had the highest morale I've ever seen in a group of employees. We were enthusiastic, dedicated to our programs and the community and, usually, very satisfied. We felt supported in our efforts by not only the sponsoring agencies but also by the federal regional office.

The administrators and sponsors of the VISTA program ran it wisely, allowing us full autonomy. As a result, we accomplished amazing feats with limited financial resources. The VISTA program was an example of an organization that knew how to promote high levels of employee satisfaction, enthusiasm, trust and respect.

The good news is, when we already know how to create these positive feelings in our personal lives, we have at least a clue about how the process works. We can see that treating people well, listening to them and managing them with trust and respect leads to returned enthusiasm, respect and loyalty. The bad news is, when we don't know how to create and maintain positive feelings in our own lives, we find ourselves up to our necks in problems and confusion when we try to manage others.

Human behavior is extraordinarily complex because it arises out of our individual sets of experiences and our ever-changing moods. Trying to sort out this confusion without self-understanding is an impossible task. But when you understand that _the behavior you want follows the feelings you create_—in yourself and others—you have the ability to resolve a myriad of management problems, no matter what behaviors are at cause. Without this knowledge, all the education, workshops and training in the world won't help because the problem is a function of low self-understanding manifested in negative feelings, _not_ information to be learned.

The beauty of seeing the connection between feelings and behavior is that we're saved from drowning in the details of our employees' problems. Dealing with employees (or anybody else for that matter) involves the same common sense that we usually reserve for children.

My nephew is five years old and rides an emotional rollercoaster. When he's mad at his parents or me, he pouts, stomps and yells. If I didn't understand that his outbursts are the result of his _very_ temporary low moods, I'd always be bewildered. However, because I feel compassion for him, even at his worst, I use common sense. Sometimes I listen, sometimes I don't. The nature of his complaint doesn't make a particle of difference. Sometimes I'm patient, sometimes I draw a hard line. My response is always tempered because I know his behavior will change with his feelings.

I have enough understanding to know that children in low moods say and do unpleasant things. The same principle holds true in the workplace—when your employees' feelings change, so will their behavior.

You and your employees should follow the dictates of

your common sense from the framework of your own positive feelings. Often, what it takes to change negative feelings to positive ones is a break—an opportunity to relax and quiet the mind. In other words, your problem-solving abilities are better when you and your employees feel good. When the boss recognizes that you're burned out and recommends you take a vacation, he's applying this wisdom. When an employee has a harrowing morning and takes a break to allow her stress to dissipate, she's applying this common sense. Both recognize that their feelings are getting in the way of their performance.

In a positive work environment, we make decisions and solve problems through plain old *common sense.* The simplicity of this concept is a huge relief for those, like myself, who are perplexed by Theory X,Y,Z, Maslow's hierarchy of needs, managing-for-performance, Japanese style management, and complicated incentive and profit-sharing programs. In fact, the key to dealing with the complexity of the Information Age is to solve problems and make decisions while relying on understanding, positive feelings and common sense as guides.

Seeing that people do their best when they feel good and that negative feelings pollute our thoughts and actions is a powerful insight. Most often, our blocked vision isn't caused by the details but rather the emotional content of circumstances. Surmounting a problem by paying less attention to negative feelings comes easily to the executive who understands this. Let me illustrate this concept with a story my father tells about my grandfather:

"My father owned a large paper mill in the early 1950s. In 1952, the plant burned to the ground and there were no financial resources to rebuild it. One day, soon after the fire, the other executives and I were extremely depressed, immobile, just sitting around in the remains of the office—there was no light at the tunnel's end. While we were feeling sorry for ourselves and unable to do anything, my father stood up and grabbed a broom. He began sweeping the floor simply because it was dirty. He refused to let the situation control him. We were all astonished by his amazing ability to drop negativity and do what needed to be done."

This incident made the local newspaper because it was such a good example of personal courage, wisdom and self-understanding in the face of traumatic circumstances.

The Special Importance of Mood and Morale

There's a beautiful river park near my house. I've spent a lot of time writing in this park. I sit under a huge fir tree and watch ducks, geese and swans float up and down the river. Families feed the ducks and chat with each other. Some admire the extraordinary beauty of the setting. Others notice the duck droppings. The ones who notice the beauty are invariably in a good mood, grateful to be there. Those who focus on the duck droppings are usually in bad moods, complaining about traffic, worried about their children falling in the river or fretting over last night's dinner bill. Their bad moods dramatically alter their ability to see beauty and enjoy themselves. They genuinely experience a different reality from those whose contentment lets them enjoy beauty.

Moods are predispositions to feel positively or negatively about the world. They limit the range of feelings available to us. They represent our states of mind, determining how we see and respond to the world. And moods shape the way others respond to us.

My father employed an extremely negative manager who saw employees as shiftless and working just for the money. His attitude virtually guaranteed a "C-" effort from everyone. There was a short rise of steps between the office and the warehouse where employees stacked bags from conveyer belts. When I first worked as a bag stacker, my colleagues told me to keep an eye on the door to the office, which could be seen over the top of the stairs. You could tell when the negative manager was arriving because the office door was *open* longer; he was way out of shape and it took him significantly longer than anyone else to come through the door. When we saw the door stay open, we worked harder. We kept it up while he watched us, commenting all the while on our laziness. When he returned to the office, we slacked off. We worked faster to avoid his ire and got even by slacking off when he left. Although his negativity elicited our creativity, it was directed at beating the system rather than working harder and smarter.

On the other hand, I once worked for a social service agency whose director was in a good mood most of the time. It was a pleasure working with her. She inspired loyalty, trust and respect, and the long hours the staff put in reflected our genuine positive feelings for her and the agency.

Moods are to an individual as morale is to an organization. Morale represents the collective moods of everyone in the organization. Business productivity responds to changes in morale in the same way that personal functioning follows mood changes. Just as it's hard to function when we're depressed, an organization has trouble being productive when morale is down. In low moods, people tend to take things too personally and exaggerate the perils of the environment. We're also liable to resist change and overreact, obstructing the flow of information from the world around us. In higher moods, *we do just the opposite.* We see clearly and are open to change.

One of my favorite things about traveling in foreign countries is freeing myself of knee-jerk emotional reactions and enjoying non-stop high spirits. I was in Italy one summer, enjoying lunch at a sidewalk cafe with friends, when a man walked over to our table and began screaming at us. We couldn't understand a word he was saying. We knew only that he was extremely mad about something. As he screamed, my friends and I looked at each other and shrugged; we didn't have a clue. After a few minutes, the man threw his arms up in frustration, rolled his eyes and left.

Our experience of his hostility was mostly

puzzlement—we wondered what in the heck we were doing that was so upsetting. We were in a good mood and couldn't understand what he was saying. As a result, none of us took his tirade personally. The strongest emotion we felt was curiosity.

Had we understood what he was saying, I'm sure we would have lost our high spirits. The confrontation would have escalated. As it was, however, after the screamer left, my friends and I went on happily with our lunch.

In this situation, our good moods and the difficulty we had taking the attack personally dissipated the argument. We were glad to be in Rome on a sunny day. Since it takes two to argue, and among the four of us we were three short, there was no argument.

The same phenomenon that allowed us to listen to the screaming Italian without becoming personally involved allows a manager in a positive mood to listen to an employee vent his or her negative feelings without getting upset. *The active ingredient in our ability to listen well and communicate with others is mood.*

Towards the end of the month, cash flow was a problem in the family concrete business. During that time, we never asked my father for anything that cost money or presented him with any surprises. We knew that his mood was undermined by financial anxieties. Our requests and, in fact, *any* new ideas were in trouble before they were discussed.

Early in my career, one of my jobs required that I call on buyers. On these visits, I would start with a "mood check." Dealing with buyers who are in bad moods is like fishing for piranha while you're standing in the river. Our company recognized the validity of the mood model by calling on buyers when they were most likely to feel good. This turned out to be between 10:00 a.m. and 2:00 p.m. on Tuesday through Thursday.

Here's a good example of mood's power to boost decision-making abilities. My friend tells the story like this:

"Last June my youngest son graduated from high school. After his graduation, we went out for pizza. We pulled around the corner and a semi-truck literally ran *over* the front of our car. Fortunately no one was hurt, but the car was totaled. Because I was in a really good mood, it didn't upset me. The next day I called a car salesman friend and told him I wanted a car. I trusted him to choose the right one. He did, and the whole process was effortless despite the seriousness of the accident. I was proud of myself.

"About a month later I was very busy, working a lot of hours. I left an appointment feeling stressed, was running a little late, and scraped the side of my new car on a low brick wall hidden under some leaves. It really upset me. I was extended financially; this was the last straw. I tried to calm down, telling myself I could deal with it. But I found myself thinking the whole mess (really just a slightly scratched car and a few bills) proved that I couldn't afford my lifestyle. In my agitation, I decided to act.

"On the way to my next appointment I resolved to

sell or rent my house and move into a smaller apartment. This could free up $150 and, if I really slummed it, $200. *Then* I could afford scratched cars, broken teeth or whatever other emergencies I had to deal with. I tried to be as rational as possible, telling myself I wasn't in a bad mood (which I was) and that I was handling this (which I wasn't). To cap it off, I even got lost on the way to my next appointment.

"Everything snowballed. By the time I got back to the store, I was certain I couldn't afford my lifestyle. I called a couple of realtors to put my house on the market and told my son to make his room presentable. He cleaned up his room and started packing.

"At the time, I was working 12-14 hours a day and was exhausted. One night, after a hard day, my son reminded me we were supposed to box up the kitchen. I just couldn't do it. I was so tired I couldn't even think about it.

"Then, I sat down on the sofa and just stopped. I slowed down, relaxed, drifted into a better mood, and realized that I'd been living in a frenzy. All the decisions I'd been making weren't healthy. I saw clearly that I didn't have to do *anything* I'd planned. I really didn't need to sell my house; the car insurance would take care of the car. All I really needed was a good night's sleep."

My friend's realization that her problems were grossly overblown and that all she really need was good night's sleep is typical of the insights possible with a little understanding. The way her moods and feelings affected her ability to see solutions shows how problems virtually resolve themselves through changes in attitude. To her credit she had the courage to recognize what was happening, relax, and drop her negativity before she took drastic—and unnecessary—actions.

Low moods reflect low self-understanding. People in low moods have lost the knowledge that _their mood creates their feelings and perceptions._ In negative moods, they believe the world is a threatening place. They defend their point of view in the face of obvious reasons for changing, protecting their sense of importance when they should be considering other viewpoints. They try to control their environment when they should be loosening up.

Some organizations go through regular, predictable periods of low morale. I once worked with a resort that had a low period every off-season. Employees didn't have enough to do and worried about their jobs. This morale lull happens every year, like clockwork, and disappears as the tourists return. If this climate persisted, the company would have chronic problems. Knowing, however, that their problem is seasonal gives employees the understanding to deal with it more effectively. They don't overreact by instituting programs that create more problems than they solve. They _know_ the situation will pass. "Blue Monday" is the same phenomenon—it passes too.

In contrast to the recreation business, a small manufacturing company expects slowdowns during the holidays. During December, our family business had low sales, low cash flow, low production, bad weather, higher costs, preoccupied employees and low profit. January 1st signaled the beginning of a new, happier time. As a result, we planned for the slowdown and never overreacted to it.

Clouds Across the Sun

All of us go through different moods during the day. Mood changes don't need a reason; they blow in and out like clouds across the sun. The success of MBWA, or "management by walking around," is based on monitoring employee moods. If you find that your employees are satisfied, motivated and productive, don't fix it, it ain't broke, as the bumper sticker says. If, however, your employees are bored, grouchy or dissatisfied, you've got a morale problem.

Recognizing a morale problem and its impact on performance is as illuminating as realizing you're limping because there's a rock in your shoe. Remember, morale represents the *collective moods* of your employees. Low morale is the rock in your organizational shoes. Halting organizational performance most often comes from your employees' low moods—the rocks. Managers who realize this know it makes more sense over the long haul to deal with the rock rather than the limp.

Sometimes the only out is to buy new shoes. A business owner I'll call Ellen was having problems with her secretary/receptionist. Always in a blue funk, this secretary expected the worst in people. She was extremely defensive, believing every customer was a source of trouble. Her phone voice was flat and devoid of character. Her favorite topics of conversation were bad weather, the difficulty of finding jobs, problems with children, and the turmoil and struggle of life. She created rapport by one-upping her listener's negative experiences. Interactions with her were usually depressing. Customers complained. It became apparent she couldn't project the positive, motivated image Ellen wanted.

Ellen knew the receptionist was her company's first line of public relations and that first impressions were critical. Ellen tried with all her heart to change the employee, using every trick she knew to alter the receptionist's self-presentation. Nothing worked for more than a day or two. At the time of our meeting, Ellen was at a loss about what to do.

After my first meeting with Ellen it became apparent the employee's problems came from her consistent low mood. After discussing the role of mood in creating behavior, Ellen saw clearly that she had a significant morale problem. She also saw that the employee's low mood was out of her hands. She began to appreciate how the receptionist's negativity affected staff performance.

Simply *realizing* these facts was a breath of fresh air for Ellen. She stopped struggling to make the receptionist feel better. When Ellen relaxed, she saw the futility of continuing to hope for change. Ellen and I both agreed she had worked with the receptionist compassionately and respectfully. Their communications were clear and clean. The receptionist's ongoing negative mood was _simply unchangeable._ Ellen dismissed the receptionist, replacing her with a less qualified but more cheerful person. The results were happier customers, a better company image and a smoother running office.

Linda, John, and the salesman solved their problems in a different way. In both cases, however, solutions emerged after a jump in self-understanding. On one hand, Linda's self-understanding gave her the information she needed to work out her employee problems. On the other hand, Ellen's self-understanding gave her the courage to make a difficult decision.

Respecting high morale and the positive feelings it engenders is management's key to long-term organizational success. The business leader who appreciates this knows when his or her organization is off track. They also know whether the problem is a limp or a rock—a problem of details or a problem of mood.

The way to build positive feelings and better personal and organizational functioning is, first, to _recognize that the primary problem is one of mood or morale_ and, second, to _stop feeding the negativity._

When we're in low moods it's easy to perpetuate painful feelings through self-criticism and gossip. "I'll never get this right—I must be incredibly stupid." "Gosh I'm fat—I'll be fat the rest of my life." "What a lousy day—the world is full of greedy people." "Joe's work is awful lately—I'm sure it's because he's preoccupied with Marie." Self-understanding dissipates the effects of negative self-talk and gossip, opening the door to better feelings. By recognizing that you're in a low mood, you gain perspective about negative things you say to yourself and hear from others. This new perspective clears your head and enhances your creativity.

The rumor mill comes from and perpetuates low morale. Managers who hear rumors should know that somebody is feeding the organization's negativity and lowering performance. Short-circuiting company gossip serves the same function as refusing to fuel your own lousy moods. Without fuel morale rises. Employees return to doing their jobs rather than spinning their mental wheels. The self-rising quality of positive feelings could be called the "helium principle" because helium balloons and feelings both rise naturally when the ballast is cast off.

Positive moods and morale return when we stop feeding negativity in the same way that fresh air fills a stuffy room when we open a window. How do we go about keeping the window open—i.e. creating and maintaining good feelings?

First, recognize that *we* are the ones who open the window (change our feelings). The only way to find lasting access to the fresh air is to realize that we've closed the window and need to open it. To do this, we have to see how our own thoughts trip us up and create negative feelings. The closed window standing between us and fresh air is of our own fabrication. We create negative feelings from our own limited perspective of the world. We stubbornly hang onto our restricted viewpoint even when it doesn't serve us well. We block new information, are defensive and judgmental, take things personally and resist change. We lose sight of the fact that we are creating the harried, stressful world we live in.

Sometimes, all it takes to regain the feelings we want is to remember the link between feelings and behavior and the other simple truths of human functioning presented in this book. It's *always* possible to regain positive feelings by dropping the negativity that's keeping them alive. We are the only ones who can do that—*we* are responsible for the way we feel.

Second, we don't have to know the details of window design or construction to bring in fresh air. Likewise, we don't have to know the reasons behind our feelings and actions to get back on track. Reasons are beside the point.

It's easy to get sidetracked by the details of our problems. They're extraordinarily interesting, especially to us. However, when you approach management problems via the whos, whys, whens, whats, hows and wheres of behavior and motivation, you get stuck in a quagmire of complexity, distracted by the flotsam and jetsam of contaminated thought processes.

We can find reasons for any management problem. However, reasons are often like the tail of a comet—they stream out behind us. They're the rational for acting on our feelings. Reasons add to complexity—self-understanding cuts through it. Knowing the reasons for problems doesn't tell us how to solve them. But the degree to which we can think clearly, make decisions and solve problems depends on how well we understand how our minds work.

Third, merely realizing that the house is stuffy tells you how to solve the problem. Similarly, seeing that your management problems result from low morale gives you all you need to change. For example, one day during a slow business period, you notice that employee performance is down and the rumor mill is up and running. You immediately recognize the signs of a morale problem. In other words, the windows need opening. You don't overreact or take the circumstances personally. You don't try to control behavior by restricting breaks, installing time clocks or becoming hard-nosed. Instead, you approach your employees with respect and openness, interested in what's causing their morale drop.

By talking with employees, you find they're afraid the lack of business will cause layoffs. You discuss the situation openly and honestly, reassuring them and creating an easy, secure atmosphere. As a result, morale lifts. Employees relax and stop feeding the rumor mill. You then work together to solve the problem. You might hire temporaries during busy times to avoid layoffs during slack times, diversify into other product lines, increase sales, find ways to cut costs, ignore the slump because it's temporary, or do any of a number of things—_all a direct result of raising morale_ and freeing employee creativity.

An individual's mood and a company's morale represent _levels of functioning—how_ effective we are at seeing clearly and processing information and making decisions. Knowing this enables us to see how the people around us are doing as we become happier, more creative and compassionate, and better able to deal with whatever life and the company throw our way. Our management style becomes more inspirational because we learn how to create the positive feelings that give rise to inspiration. To reiterate, the way to restore positive feelings and a higher level of functioning is, first, to recognize low spirits and know the primary problem is one of mood or morale and, second, to stop feeding negativity. The first step takes considerable courage. When we're in low spirits we look outside ourselves for causes of our upset when, in fact, it's coming from within us. During bouts of hostility, anxiety and stress, it takes courage to remember that high motivation and performance come naturally from positive feelings, *not* negative ones. In the middle of arguments we often forget that the very fact that we're arguing means we're not hitting on all cylinders. We can still make decisions and solve problems when we're upset and when our company is full of stress, but we don't do it as well.

The second step—not feeding negativity—also takes courage. During low times it feels important to be right. As long as we're trying to prove we're right, we keep feeding the negativity generated by our fears of being wrong. Anybody who's argued for the sake of being right knows how hollow victory can feel. Feeding negativity to be right is worse than driving faster during a snowstorm because the road's slippery and you want to get home quicker.

In our plant, I used to see the following downward spiraling interaction happen all too often.

The manager, in a suspicious mood, would walk into the production area. Seeing an employee struggling with a partially sealed bag, he thinks:

Now there's an expensive mistake. Isn't that typical? You just can't get good help anymore. We can't afford to lose bags from incompetence.

He asks, thinking he already knows the answer:

"Hey, what's going on here?"

The employee says:

"The machinery isn't working right."

Thinking that the employee doesn't really care about saving the company money, he says:

"If you operated the machinery right and cared about anything but your paycheck, it wouldn't break."

The employee replies:

"We do the best we can with this old junk."

Taking the statement (mostly true) as a personal attack on his ability to manage, as well as an indication of the ingratitude of manual laborers in Los Angeles, he says:

"Here, let me do it."

Then, in his upset, he grabbed the 90-pound bag, tried to lift it to the conveyor belt to rerun it through the gluing machine. He strained his back, tore the bag and created a huge mess. Throwing his hands up in disgust, he told the employee to clean up the floor. He stomped back to the office, muttering about the worthlessness of employees in particular and young people in general. He also prepared to institute stricter hiring and training procedures so this wouldn't ever happen again. In this situation the employee feels resentful and resolves to get even. By feeding his downward spiral of negativity, the manager successfully turned a simple production glitch (caused in large part by antiquated equipment) into a major personnel problem.

To reiterate an important point, personal moods and organizational morale are as changeable as the weather but, if released from the weight of the negativity that holds them down, *they'll rise as high as we're willing to let them go*. It takes *active effort* to stay negative. The manager above shoveled negativity into his mind like coal into a furnace, oblivious to its self-fulfilling nature.

Managing by State of Mind:
The Reset Button

I sang in a choir for years. It strikes me that managing employees is very much like leading a singing group. When the bass singers are out of sync with the sopranos, it's better to start over rather than hope the harmonies will self-correct.

Correcting productivity problems can also entail beginning afresh. It works something like the reset button on a garbage disposal, a mechanism that enables you to restart the system when it jams rather than replacing it.

It makes little practical sense to get rid of employees as a knee-jerk reaction to poor performance. Your organizational climate comes from employees' combined moods. Changing employees, like changing singers in a discordant choir, isn't effective in the long run. *Employee performance depends on climate, and organizational climate starts with management's mood.*

For example, if a music director, ignorant of the way his lousy mood spoils his leadership abilities, flies into a rage every time a soprano makes mistakes, he or she will create the very problem that's trying to be corrected. The singers will become anxious and make more errors. Replacing singers won't help since the real problem is the director's mood. Similarly, managers with little appreciation of the role their own moods play will find managing others frustrating. They'll likely create stress and poor performance in people who will really perform better by loosening up.

Your fundamental leadership role, then, is *managing your state of mind and that of your employees.* You and your employees do your best when you can use your intelligence and training in a positive, supportive work environment. Understanding the significance and function of state of mind (morale) is the essence of good management and your organizational reset button. When you see how it works, you manage others well because you understand how to reset negativity to positivity. Remember, high performance follows high spirits.

Here's another important point about managing by state of mind. Managers need a certain amount of technical know-how to lead employees, just as choir directors need musical expertise to lead musicians. The amount of expertise that they need, however, is less than you might think.

Morale is the underlying force that determines how technical expertise is used. It is, therefore, at the core of productivity. Employees in high spirits will use the knowledge they have more effectively, learn more easily and be more productive than their gloomier colleagues. As a result, it makes sense to evaluate prospective employees' mental well-being as well as technical expertise when hiring. It makes more sense to have your car repaired by a content mechanic rather than an angry one. The difference shows up in the quality of work and the size of the bill. I advise my career counseling clients to seek companies that seem happy places to work because positive companies treat their people fairly and with respect.

Management's state of mind filters down through

organizations rapidly. Insecure managers hire insecure employees who then deal with each other and customers in defensive, insecure ways. Secure, positive managers who appreciate how they contribute to their own moods hire secure people who make difficult decisions easily, work together well and are of service to customers.

For example, an east coast company has an internal policy that managers should fire or discipline only when they are in a good mood. This reflects upper management's understanding that when you're in a good mood, you see clearly and act appropriately. You take difficult actions (like firing someone) in a clear-headed, compassionate way that serves employees and the company. Employees naturally serve each other and customers when they feel good about themselves and their role in the company. Managing by inspiration involves generating creative enthusiasm in ourselves and our people. It depends on recognizing that moods and morale are real and powerful forces, not abstractions or humanistic fluff.

Organizational morale rises naturally in a climate of mutual respect, trust and cooperation. We sometimes think that morale can be pumped up like a deflated tire. However, the never-ending chore of morale-boosting exhausts even tireless managers. Seeing that productivity and motivation come naturally from positive feelings—which grow when we stop feeding negative thoughts and behaviors—is blessedly simple. And it steers managers toward the right actions to take, policies to explore, and strategies to use in working with employees.

High spirits are an incredible gift that grease the

wheels of organizational productivity as they smooth out relationships. As we begin to see where they come from and learn how to nurture them, they assume a larger presence in life. Have faith in your personal positive moods and your organization's high morale; they'll help you prosper more than anything else. And the more you come to rely on them, the better they'll serve you.

Chapter 3

Self-Image and Insecurity:
Dragging Performance Down

How does the ego work against successful relationships and business results?

Ever since we were young, we've been told it's better to be one way than another. It's better to be smart than dumb, successful than a failure, congenial than disagreeable, on time than late, happy than sad, rich than poor, active than lazy, skinny than fat, strong than weak, generous than stingy—the list is as endless as there are people and values. From these values, passed down through our parents, grandparents and peers, we learn to judge life. We learn to assess what's happening around us and how to feel about what we see, hear and taste.

Most of the time our values lie under the surface of our consciousness like the submerged body of an iceberg. We use this vast mass of stored information to see and interpret each other, the world and ourselves. Because our values shape the way we think, they are the basis for our idea of who we are—*our self-image or ego.* We may define ourselves as intelligent, shy, punctual, thin, witty, humble, cheerful, compassionate, macho, pragmatic, thrifty, physically fit, humorous—each of us has a vast network of these mental filters stored in memory. Composed of the qualities we ascribe to ourselves, they help to determine how we perceive the world. Although there are commonalities among culture and gender, self-images differ dramatically from person to person.

Self-images determine the activities we prefer. If you don't think this pertains to the workplace, try to start an incentive program without asking your employees what they want. For example, a client of mine once tried to motivate his sales staff through a contest. The winner would receive a trip to the west coast, all expenses paid. The contest didn't produce the desired results because, unfortunately, many of the company's top performers thought of themselves as sportsmen and hunters. They didn't give a hoot about spending an intimate weekend by the sea during deer hunting season.

Our values and self-images are part of us. However, the way we use them depends on our mood. During low moods, we resurrect memories and learned beliefs to try to deal with life. When we're stressed, burned out, angry or depressed, we use our egos and values like grappling hooks, desperately trying to grab and control the people and events that feel threatening and out of control. In better moods, we lighten up, treating our self-images and values with humor and understanding. Problems are resolved with common sense and wisdom. Life flows easily.

My father used to be a perfectionist. Eventually, he gave it up as a bad habit. At one time, however, he believed there was a very specific right way to act and he expected his kids to deliver. I learned the same value system and created misery for myself and those around me. In my adolescence, I lacked the wisdom to see that my interacting mood and thoughts caused my uneasy feelings. I felt controlled by my perfectionist values. When my spirits were low, I viewed what anybody did as success or failure, right or wrong, perfect or flawed. My value system had me by the throat.

Fortunately, like my father, I learned to give perfectionism the boot. I saw the intimate connection between my moods and the anxious feeling that comes with the drive to repeat actions until they're _right_. Now, the only time I feel I'm not doing something right is when I'm in a bad mood.

A client of mine sometimes forgets the connection between her compulsion to be congenial (a learned value) and her low moods. As a result, when she's in a negative state of mind, she sometimes acts sweet when she should be decisive. As her self-understanding increases, she knows how to break this cycle by paying less attention to the insecurity she's creating.

Another client is driven in low moods by his "I _am_ the boss" self-image. As a result, he has trouble delegating, thereby creating tremendous stress. Distrusting his plant foreman, he spends way too much time monitoring his 60-plus employees and supervising plant operations. The foreman's lackluster performance stems directly from the owner's unwillingness to trust him and transfer responsibility.

The driving force behind the negativity we feel in low moods is _the insecurity that comes when our self-image is threatened._ Values, beliefs and judgments are only important to us when we activate them. And we _only_ activate them to try to make sense of the world when our spirits are low and our ego is under attack. Ego and insecurity are like a pair of sleeping lions; wake up one and you'll be battling both.

Whenever we feel good—relaxed in a hot shower, on vacation, viewing a favorite television program, watching our children sleep, skiing fresh powder on a beautiful day or doing absolutely nothing and just enjoying life—common sense tells us to ignore the beliefs and judgments that invariably pop up. During these times, we recognize them for what they are— negative thoughts born of ego with little or no value to us.

Clearly, values and beliefs don't always serve us well. When our moods are low even "good" values can get in the way of our seeing anything new, adapting to change and responding to the unusual with creativity and freshness. Managing by inspiration depends on our ability to still our belief systems and be open to new information. When we're defending threatened beliefs we can't be open.

Positive attributes are always present when we're in good moods. They only disappear when we are afraid of losing them. For example, I had a client who couldn't manage effectively because he was afraid to appear mean. He was caught between a rock and a hard place. From his point of view, he was either too nice or too blunt. As he came to understand how values affect self-image, he developed a more relaxed, broader range of responses. As he began to see that his difficulties were due to his threatened sense of self-importance in low moods, he paid less attention to his fears. Ironically, as he dropped the self-image that drove him to be congenial at any cost, he became more congenial than ever before. When we begin to see how we contribute to our own negativity, we lighten up. We become more of everything good that we worry we've lost when we're upset.

The quality of niceness that my client prized is genuine when it is a by-product of self-understanding. But when positive qualities are part of our egos, they disappear when that ego is threatened. When our sense of who we are fastens to a belief and that belief is threatened, we feel anxiety and anger. These are hardly the kinds of feelings that promote good decision-making and problem-solving. When self-images come under attack, we feel most feelings *except* those that enable us to manage effectively. An essential part of self-understanding is seeing how our egos block positive feelings, the source of positive behaviors. Most threats to the self-image pass by quickly because we recognize how silly they are. Ego-generated insecurity only causes problems when it hooks us and we start feeding the negative thoughts that come with it. For example, I had lunch recently with Wayne, a friend who was having trouble communicating with his father. Every time they talked about controversial issues, Wayne, who was in his late twenties, felt like a little kid. He desperately defended his viewpoints, as shaky as even *he* thought they were, and felt like an idiot.

Hampered by a threatened self-image and activated insecurities, Wayne's interactions with his father got worse and worse. This, of course, made his father believe he was right about Wayne's incompetence. He became aggressive and accusatory, seeing his own failings in his son as his lifelong fears of being incompetent were activated. And so it went, on and on—a discussion between competing egos isn't a pretty sight.

Arguments always have an element of offended ego at their core. The problem was that neither son nor father understood the dynamics of self-image and fear. If they had, they would have refused to sustain this downward spiral. The fact is, when you know enough to catch yourself defending your ego, you lighten up. And, when you lighten up, you communicate better.

Many of us are motivated by anger and act out of self-righteousness. However, in pumping up our egos to create the illusion of being right, we decrease our flexibility (in case we're actually wrong) and compassion (in case the other side has merit, which it almost always does). Interventions are best carried out in a calm, non-blaming and non-judgmental climate.

Employer/employee relationships can become like the destructive relationship between Wayne and his father. When employees are an extension of your self-image or values and they act in ways violating that image, it is as if a child has disgraced the family name and you, personally, are threatened.

For about a year, I was the administrative coordinator for a national marketing cooperative comprised of male-dominated, family-owned businesses. The owners of these companies treated their grown sons and daughters as an extension of their own value systems. The owners/fathers took everything the adult children did personally. The same dynamics can hold true between employer and employee, owner and manager, and supervisor and production worker, although the phenomenon isn't as glaring as in closely held firms. If you're taking it personally, your ego's activated. Watch out! A manager's threatened self-image really limits his or her effectiveness.

Despite these examples, employees' egos are more often threatened by management than vice-versa. This makes sense when you consider all that the boss can take away—power, income, prestige, independence and even the job itself. This is also why the morale in an organization trickles down faster than it trickles up—and why it's so important for upper management to have a high level of self-understanding.

Threatened egos cause insecurity—the fear that we're in danger or that something is about to be taken away. Recognizing insecurity in the workplace and diffusing it is an important management function. Managers with self-understanding know that most negative feelings come from their threatened egos. When they're insecure, they know enough to pay less attention to their thoughts and to act with caution because their decision-making abilities are hampered. They also know that their employees respond to insecurity in the same way—when they feel threatened, they're insecure and performance is likely to suffer.

Insecurity in the workplace is the primary cause of conflict. For example, my family company once made the mistake of promoting a truck driver to plant supervisor when we knew he was often insecure, had personality conflicts with another driver and sometimes solved problems with his fists.

The new supervisor and the other driver despised each other and had tangled verbally in the past. Promoting one of them exacerbated the situation. During an argument, when our new supervisor's competence was threatened, he punched the other driver, who fell backwards and struck his head on a forklift tine—an injury that resulted in a large medical claim. If we had recognized the extent of the promoted driver's insecurity—or if he had had enough self-understanding to recognize when his insecurity had him by the throat— the mess would have never occurred.

Our self-images aren't resilient, strong and flexible; rather, they are brittle, resistant to change and vulnerable to threat. When they are attacked, we feel insecure and go into defense mode. But you know what? There's no physical danger. In fact, self-image is nothing more than a story spun of ideas and beliefs, as illusory as the Emperor's new clothes. When we can see we've made it all up, we can stop taking ourselves quite as seriously.

I've been an avid skier for more than 30 years. Many times I've taken a tumble and come up laughing. Sometimes, however, I get caught up in the image of myself as "mountain master." When this happens, I ski as much for other skiers as for myself. Occasionally, if my ego is exceptionally active (if I'm showing off), I'll be angry after a good fall under the chairlift—angry at myself, angry at the spectators above, angry at my bindings—just plain angry, certain that somebody or something is to blame. It's all baloney. When I ski for the joy of it, a fall is just a fall and has no meaning. It's my activated mountain master self-image and insecurity that ruins my joy of skiing.

Ego and Addictions

On one ski trip I hurt myself and was in considerable pain. You know what my first reaction was after the pain died down? I was relieved—not because the pain had eased, but because I knew I didn't have to ski anymore that season. I had been addicted to the idea that I _needed_ skiing to feel good about myself. My ego actually compelled me to ski when I would rather have stayed home.

When your mood is low and your self-image activates, you think good feelings come from outside yourself. When you become convinced that a job, sport, drug or food is the source of your good feelings, you become addicted to it. When your mood is high and you feel good, on the other hand, you _prefer_ certain activities but aren't addicted to them. You don't _depend_ on them for your self-esteem or happiness. You don't feel compulsive.

An activated ego creates the feeling of addiction. Realizing this lets you lighten up about the parts of life, including your job or business, you feel compulsive about. Workaholics are addicted to the idea that their self-esteem depends on working and achievement. When you see this compulsion as caused by a threatened self-image, it loses its grip.

Managers can become addicted to company policies in the same way that individuals can become addicted to drugs. The unwillingness to throw out dated, ineffective pricing schedules, compensation programs, dress codes or corporate goals indicates an addiction. When self-image is tied to an organization and is activated through threat, imagined or otherwise, behaviors are compulsive and defensive.

In my family's drymix concrete plant we employed a production manager who was addicted to his own macho self-image. He saw himself as the hardest-working, most loyal, smartest SOB in the plant and, as a result, never let himself or anyone else relax or make a mistake. His rigid self-image meant he could never entertain the notion that employees just might work hard, be loyal and work smart without constant nagging and threatening. He interpreted relaxing as laziness and disloyalty. It was a tough way to live and I'm sure it led to his high blood pressure, overeating and heart disease.

Someone who enjoys and *prefers* success, but isn't addicted to it, knows that success is only as good as the feelings that come along with it. Feelings of contentment and fulfillment are part and parcel of a life driven by self-understanding, not addiction to achievement. Achievement and success, like congeniality in a previous example, are the natural by-product of high spirits and morale.

The feeling of anxiety that comes with an attack on self-image is the first clue that we're misusing our ability to think. When I feel a nibbling in my chest, I know my mountain master self-image is activated. I'm about to do something from fear and insecurity rather than joy. When somebody cuts me off on the highway, a feeling of anxiety (followed quickly by anger) is a sure sign that I've taken the action personally.

Negative feelings are infallible indicators that our self-image is threatened (How dare you!), our ability to think clearly is compromised, and we're about to do something unwise. Instead of using our minds to make decisions and solve problems in a creative and respectful way, we're using them to defend and justify our beliefs.

Fear, insecurity and anxiety are powerful feelings, and they are usually misplaced. Ninety-nine percent of the time they're based on nonsensical interpretations of the world and a lack of understanding. They're caused by _perceived_ threats to an artificial self-image.

Self-Confidence:
A Paradox

Self-confidence wasn't a problem when I was a child. I enjoyed my life. I felt strong and wise without naming those feelings. We're all born with strong self-esteem.

Our self-confidence is highest when the ego is quiet. When our ego activates, we're vulnerable to threats and caught up in proving ourselves. Our active ego stands directly _between_ us and self-esteem.

It's true that boosted egos can feel good. However, because those feelings are based on the temporary relief of insecurity, our pleasure is short-lived. The same principle holds true for intense excitement, which feels good but is stressful; its effects are temporary and addictive and it has a brittle, agitated quality.

When we're not pumping up our self-images and our understanding level is high, our self-confidence is also very high—naturally. The manager who recognizes this distinction promotes policies that discourage intense internal competitiveness and encourages cooperation, respect and trust.

I once helped organize a treasure hunt for a group of children. We used coins for treasure. The other organizers and I hid quarters in different places and drew maps. The game worked as we'd planned for about one minute. Then the children realized that getting to the hiding places first meant getting all the money. We had a mob scene on our hands. There was no cooperation, only competition. The oldest and strongest ran over the youngest and weakest, who were frustrated to tears. It was an example of Darwinian survival-of-the-fittest theory applied to party games. We all learned a lot about the disadvantages of promoting competition at the expense of cooperation.

Without self-understanding, managers often activate insecurity unknowingly. For example, my friend, Andrea, was the human relations manager for a large, international company that held its employees in high esteem. One of her supervisors realized the value of promoting cooperation, respect and trust; the other did not.

Andrea's first supervisor, Robert, valued his employees highly, was very upbeat and had worked for the company a long time. He was committed to his employees' personal development. He wanted them to trust their own judgment and "do the right thing" —i.e. know the rules, know company intentions, but deviate from them when they get in the way of service and excellence. Andrea enjoyed working with Robert and was never afraid to tell him what she'd done that wasn't by the book. Andrea loved her job and excelled.

Fred, on the other hand, was very task oriented, focused on the product and worried about sticking to company policy. Andrea avoided Fred whenever she did something outside the rules. Fred's lack of understanding prevented the synergy of cooperation Andrea had had with Robert. By not realizing that his own fears created employee insecurity, Fred reduced his managerial effectiveness.

Self-Image, Security and the Workplace

The work environment that serves businesses best is one in which employees feel secure and rewarded for performance. In this environment, people don't feed each other's fears and insecurities and don't feel threatened by management policy or actions. Remember, feelings (and performance) rise as far as we let them when we stop fueling negativity.

Policies that protect against discrimination and harassment can reflect management's desire to make the work environment secure (as well as legal). Involving employees in policy formation and in hiring means you trust their opinions—making them feel more secure. Opening your doors to your employees can make them feel valued and respected. Guaranteeing jobs makes people feel safer. Tying compensation to performance can make employees feel more in control of their incomes.

All companies are different, and what reduces insecurity in one may not work in another. Whatever form they take, however, policies that reduce insecurity are a by-product of management's self-understanding. They are honest reflections of mutual respect and trust between management and employees. They are a part of management's sincere desire to help employees do their jobs—to be in service to them. They result in increased performance.

Companies that trust and respect their employees encourage them to take responsibility and make decisions that reflect a desire to serve. Without that trust and respect from above, employees won't stick their necks out for customers' benefit.

For example, after an excellent dinner at a very good restaurant our waiter told us we could order dessert in the adjacent lounge. However, when we settled into the lounge and asked for dessert, the hostess said she couldn't oblige us. It was against restaurant policy to take silverware from the kitchen to the bar. We then asked if we could order takeout desserts to eat in the bar. She said yes, so we ordered cheesecake to go. When we picked up the takeout order, however, I noticed there wasn't any silverware. When I asked for forks, the hostess explained that although she could let us eat dessert in the lounge, she still couldn't give us any silverware. By now we were getting upset (egos activating) and asked to see the manager. He listened, apologized for the misunderstanding and gave us the forks immediately.

The logistics here were simple. The *real problem* was the restaurant's policy on allowing employees to use their own judgment to serve customers. Management's lack of trust made the hostess afraid to override restaurant policy, and her fear made it difficult to satisfy her customers. The result was an insecure hostess and upset customers.

We begin our business careers trusting employees and customers. Then someone steals, returns merchandise nine months after they purchase it, lies or files an unjust stress claim. Our trust erodes, to be replaced by cynicism. In overreacting to these violations of trust, however, many people forget how liberating it can be to adopt a "have faith in God, but tie your camel" attitude. Most of our loss of trust has to do with activated egos. We get angry because we take the employee or customer's negative action personally. But, stealing and lying are *rarely* personal.

Yes, it's wise to set up policies that discourage theft, absenteeism and drug abuse. It's futile, however, to try to regulate these issues entirely with rules and time clocks. Using the camel metaphor, it's easy to become so concerned with the strength of the rope, the number of knots and the length of the line that you forget to feed the animal and it dies.

Employees do their best and work for your

company's benefit when they feel respected and trusted, secure in their roles and rewarded for performance. An organizational climate that supports these positive characteristics is creative and flexible, willing to take chances, try new approaches and bend the rules for the benefit of the business. Some of my father's most productive strategizing took place during lunch with the manager of the neighboring asphalt plant, a close friend. In the quiet, secure semi-darkness of their favorite restaurant they tackled problems, sold companies, designed product lines and created new marketing strategies. They were prudent but fearless in the safety of this warm, familiar place. They dreamed and planned on restaurant napkins.

All of us are most creative when we're secure and unjudged. One reason brainstorming works so well is because participants put aside judgments about new ideas. The result is a burst of creativity and inspiration.

Traditional management lore has it that we need a little stress, excitement and insecurity in our lives to work our hardest and achieve the most. Many times I've heard executives say, "So-and-so just isn't hungry enough to do a good job." There's a grain of truth here. Certainly, fear is a motivator. Fear will keep you in the office until 10 p.m. working on a project. It will keep your lunch breaks short and your workdays long. Fear will also keep you awake nights. It will make you treat other people poorly. Fear will cause you to take risks that are unwise and will keep you from making reasonable, appropriate decisions. Fear as a motivator is a double-edged sword: in the short run it motivates but in the long run it destroys. Companies that encourage individual performance but don't provide job security promote anxiety, stress and high turnover. In environments where fear is the major motivator, employees perform at high levels temporarily and then burn out.

Organizations with security and respect as cornerstones of the corporate culture are inspiring places to work. Managers with self-understanding are inspiring people to work for. There is a path that takes leaders past motivating by fear, discipline and power. It's the same path that teaches them how to create organizations where employees enjoy their work and respect each other. It's the path of self-understanding presented in this book.

Chapter 4

The Past

How does what happened in the past hamper my organization's progress?

The other day I got into a mild tiff with a friend over something so trivial I can't even remember what it was, except that it involved the dishwasher. Most of the conflicts in my life are as silly as this one:

Situation...

> *The dishes are clanking loudly in the dishwasher.*

My friend said:

> *"There you go again, stacking the dishes wrong in the dishwasher. You never put them in straight. They sound like they'll break any minute."*

I said:

> *"Oh come on, they haven't broken yet. You're just complaining, like you always do when I don't do things your way."*

I thought:

> *"Quick, Allan, what are some memories that'll make you right? Ah, here's a good one: earlier today, she complained about my leaving newspapers all over the kitchen table."*

I said:

> *"You complain more than anyone I know. Just a few hours ago you were griping about my leaving newspapers on the table. And that reminds me, yesterday you were complaining about..."*

And on and on...

A little way into the argument something wonderful happened. As I stood there, upset over the dishes, arguing, I saw I was digging up memories to fuel the argument so I could be right.

I thought:

> *"Uh, oh. Wait a second, Allan. Look what you're doing! You're keeping this silly argument going by unearthing old issues. You're giving them life by paying attention to them!"*

A veil lifted from my eyes. Here I was, feeding a stupid argument with obsolete information. The wind left my sails and I stopped cold. My anger melted and I felt relief, knowing I didn't have to defend myself anymore.

The real issue had nothing to do with the dishes. Rather, I was fueling my ego with memories to make myself right. Arguments have momentum in the same way shopping carts do. When you stop pushing them, they drift a little to the right or left and stop.

Memory:
Misused and Abused

Our memories are a source of very useful information—how to read, where we parked the car, and whether or not we left the bathtub water running. They're also a wellspring of wonderful feelings when we recall the people, times and places we've enjoyed. The past is a quicksand bog, however, for those who don't understand its pitfalls.

Two marriage-related executives—the senior vice president of sales and the plant manager—in our family's company were so bitter towards each other that they didn't speak at work unless they had a specific job to do. The problem began during a strike a decade earlier when cement was in short supply and they disagreed about whose customers were more important. The sales manager thought his favorite customers should be served first and the plant manager thought his were more important. Although the strike had been over for years, they fought on and on until one of them passed away. These enemies had carried their anger and mutual dislike into the present like a huge weight, fueling it endlessly with old memories. How pointless!

When we drag our memory of the past into the present, it colors the way we see the world, act and feel. It also affects the way we deal with the people around us. When we're angry or frustrated, we misuse our memories to defend and justify old positions. There's no space for anything new when our world's full of negative memories. The misuse of memory hurts us, our relationships, our employees and our business as we create a hostile environment where understanding withers.

For example, my father acquired our drymix manufacturing company primarily because the two owners wouldn't drop the past. Theirs was the first drymix plant in Southern California—an enviable position. However, their market share had eroded dramatically over 20 years. They refused to lower prices in the face of competition. As other plants moved into the area, the partners stubbornly maintained their high prices as a matter of pride and ego. They watched their business disappear, began squabbling and eventually disliked each other intensely. Based on their memories, they were first and best. But memory no longer served. By the time my father bought the firm, there were several competing drymix companies, some launched by disgruntled former employees. Being addicted to old memories—in this case past glory and high prices— destroys the ability to adapt to the present. Your past, my past and everybody else's consists entirely of memories carried into the present. We trust these memories to make decisions and solve problems, not appreciating that they're just a bunch of stored thoughts about our personal history. When we, our employees or our organizations get stuck in the past, we perpetuate problems because there's no room for anything new.

When we can see and appreciate that our memories are old news, just stored thoughts, and that they affect us only when we nurture them with our feelings and attention, we misuse them less. We also don't cut ourselves off from inspiration and common sense.

Dropping the Past

At lunch recently, a friend told me about problems she was having with a co-worker. As Kim talked she became more and more upset, thinking about all the past conflicts she had had with this person. It was clear she was dragging negative memories into the present and giving them life with her attention and feelings. Kim became more and more frustrated. Soon she was filled to the brim with negative memories of the past.

Fortunately, the waitress stopped at our table, asked us how we were doing and broke Kim's train of thought. A few seconds later a woman who resembled someone Kim adored walked by the table. Kim talked in glowing terms about how this woman had affected her life, how wonderful she was and how much she cared about her.

The change was dramatic. My friend became quieter, more understanding about her co-worker and more fun to be with—all in a matter of seconds. Dropping her negative memories created new alternatives and solutions in an instant.

We usually have the wisdom to see when *other* people's memories are interfering with their lives. Although it's more difficult to accept the responsibility for our *own* negative memories, as we begin to see the past as a silly fabrication that we often misuse, we can laugh about it. When we see others misusing the past, we're less likely to take it seriously. We notice how real memories feel and how unreal they actually are. And our compassion and tolerance deepen as we realize that nobody misuses the past on purpose.

The Past and the Work Environment

When we're around the same people every day, it becomes easy to fix them in the past, not allowing for change and growth. We often put co-workers, spouses and friends into categories—the "here comes old so-and-so" syndrome. Sometimes we don't let people be their best because we're stuck remembering who they were yesterday or last week. For example, you could count on our plant manager to be as confrontational and argumentative as he was loyal and hard-working. If he'd suddenly become cheerful and trusting, it would have flustered us. We depended on his negativity to feel better by comparison ("At least I'm not as grouchy as old so-and-so…").

The wife of a friend of mine left him. During his divorce, we always talked about his problems. After a while, I stopped enjoying his company. After a month or two, though, I saw that he needed to _forget_ about his divorce and I needed to stop defining him by his problems. I stopped commiserating. From that point on, our conversations drifted away from divorce and we started having fun. He told me that even though it sometimes felt good to get things off his chest, he was relieved to stop feeling compelled to talk about his ex-wife.

Rehashing negative memories creates a stuck and hostile present. After arguments fueled by negative memories we feel mostly relief—like when we stop hitting ourselves on the head with a hammer. It feels good by contrast in the same way that a warm room feels good when we're wet and cold. Appreciating how we misuse memories is like not hitting our heads or getting wet in the first place.

When you're thinking about your employees in negative terms, using memories to support your position, realize that you're making it difficult to find solutions in the present. In a hostile environment, discussions degenerate into debates and then into arguments. The ability to listen sinks lower and lower until _nobody_ listens. Cooling off periods work because they provide a chance to drop ego-fueling negative memories and see the situation from a fresh perspective. When our ability to be fresh is undermined by negative memories, self-understanding is what helps us to stop feeding negativity and loosen up.

We're surrounded by examples of what happens when we give life to negative memories. The plant manager in our family business hung onto his past as a way to survive the present. According to him, almost everything was better in the old days. Employees worked harder, equipment was sturdier and the world was a better place. He used his tough-time memories (ten miles uphill in the snow) to gauge quality and set standards for himself and his employees. This invariably led to anxiety and stress. He never dropped his negative past and hadn't a clue about what it was doing to him and everybody else.

Working with the same people, day after day, it's easy to expect them to act and talk the same way. By freeing those around us from our negative memories and stereotypes, however, we open the door to creativity— from them and from us. Seeing people in the present makes them less inclined to hold *themselves* in the past, too.

The negative past raises its ugly head in insecure environments. If your corporate values promote intense internal competition, they'll also foster defensive behavior that's rooted in the past and fueled by anxiety. You'll find that people tend to rehash the same old topics in meetings. Fear inhibits creativity. For example, there's a local business association that, until recently, had a reputation for being difficult to work with. They subscribed to the "We've already tried that" approach. Whenever they discussed new marketing, advertising and even simple building decorating ideas, inevitably someone said, "That'll never work, we tried it before." It didn't matter that they'd tried it a long time ago. Since it had been tried once and failed to work, they *knew* it couldn't work now. As a result, they didn't accomplish anything.

If, on the other hand, your company encourages teamwork through cooperation, mutual respect and supportive creativity, your employees will be open to new ideas and less anchored to the past, and your goals will be ambitious yet achievable. Staff meetings in a family planning agency I worked for were a pleasure. We valued creativity and had high mutual trust and respect. Our goals were flexible and realistic because they were developed in a supportive atmosphere with the organization's vision in mind.

Plans and actions based on negative memories are often ineffective because they arise from a restricted, self-protective view of the world. When we're upset, we're closed to new ideas and change. Arguments reflect inflexibility and misuse of memory. Next time you're upset, notice how you're using memories to make yourself right at any cost. Hanging onto the past hampers decision-making. When a manager pays less attention to his kneejerk reaction to old so-and-so's lateness, predictability in meetings and dislike of sales or production, he begins loosening up in the present so he can see the employee from a fresh perspective. Old so-and-so may indeed have behaviors that hamper performance. However, feeding negativity by rehashing old memories won't help. The manager needs to free himself from his own mental debris before he can develop effective solutions.

The loosening-up process is what happened to me in the dishwasher argument. It's also what happened to the owner of the high-tech company in the first chapter when she began to see the salesman differently. This new perspective leads first to feelings of understanding and then to new alternatives and solutions. The change can be dramatic. To the extent you and your employees can forget the past as you work together, you'll enable everyone to be as innovative as they can possibly be.

Remember, the past is only stored thought. It has no substance by itself. However, when you bring negative stored thoughts into the present, creating negative feelings, you compromise the quality of your thinking and your ability to respond to new circumstances. When you perpetuate a negative organizational climate, you do the same—compromise the ability of your organization to adapt. The two partners who refused to drop their prices in the face of competition are an example of how this mindset can destroy a company.

Corporate retreats work when they enable participants to *derail* negative thoughts perpetuated in the work environment. If management doesn't understand how employees maintain negative thoughts and feelings, however, the good effects of retreats don't last and conflicts and morale problems recur.

Dropping the past enables us to use common sense to *live in the present and plan for the future.* Dropping our memories lets us use common sense to solve problems instead of creating fertile soil for further complications. Dropping the past leads to strength in the present, *not weakness.* It delivers the courage needed to make firm, compassionate business decisions.

The past is useful as a source of facts and as a stimulus for creating warm, positive feelings in the present. It is _never_ useful as justification for being right or protecting an unproductive viewpoint.

Forgetting the past when it doesn't create positive feelings like compassion, trust and respect is the key to satisfying employee relationships and good performance. Dropping the past as an excuse for poor performance or chronic ill will frees up tremendous energy, giving rise to creativity, cooperation and more of the common sense that solves problems and makes businesses and relationships successful.

Chapter 5

Something from Nothing

How does thinking create different realities?

The business world is oriented towards results. Self-understanding, or knowledge of how our minds work, influences our daily productivity and, therefore, our ability to produce results.

The first four chapters of this book addressed how feelings and moods, self-images and memory make all the difference in personal and organizational performance. Now let's turn to the source of these functions. When we start a business, we're creating something from nothing. Stop for a second and consider how a mere dream takes on physical form. We expend energy acquiring the buildings, employees, company cars, office furniture, laptop computers, manufacturing equipment, delivery trucks, inventory, paperclips and ferns that make up a company to manifest a simple idea, a thought. Without that idea, we'd never put together a business plan, borrow the money, build the warehouse, lease the retail space, hire the employees or buy the manufacturing equipment.

Our power to maintain these physical entities on a day-to-day basis depends on our clarity of thought and problem-solving ability, which are directly influenced by our feelings, moods and morale. Creating and maintaining a business is, therefore, always connected to mental functioning—our thinking.

In fact, we create something out of nothing all the time, *via our thoughts.* Whether we're forming a company, cooking a meal, painting a house, starting a relationship, writing a report or mowing a lawn, making something out of our thoughts is really what we're doing.

Many physical things around us are products of our thoughts. This is fairly easy to see. We imagine things and make them happen. However, we're less aware that our self-images, values, feelings and memories are also thought-created—maybe because we're so close to them. Our memories are stored thoughts. Our self-images are learned values animated by thought. Our feelings are the result of how we interpret circumstances—what we think. The message is clear: *our thinking creates our life experience.*

Organizations grow from the thoughts and states of minds (moods) of their people. No matter how solid or big they are, they're still thought-created. This is why organizations change so dramatically with new management. As the new managers' values, memories and moods filter down through companies, change follows.

Realizing that organizations are produced by thought is a wonderfully freeing insight. Your company's hardware and software (bricks and human resources) are a product of thinking, which in turn is shaped by moods. When this becomes clear, you no longer have to search for the answer to managerial problems, which almost always involve negative feelings, misuse of the thinking process and a lack of understanding.

Laughing It Off

Research shows that humor plays an important role in the workplace, increasing our ability to organize data and be productive. When we're lighthearted, we're less liable to waste time defending our egos or viewpoints. Here's an underlying fact: humor helps us to treat our thoughts and feelings less seriously—as if they were less true and had less value. And, when we do this, our lives work better, we make clearer decisions, and solve our problems more easily. Organizations are the same way. When managers are lighthearted, employees are less serious, morale problems are fleeting and decisions come more easily.

Management theory is beginning to recognize the importance of positive humor in the workplace. (Positive and negative humor are different. Laughter that results from ego-driven ridicule or sarcasm offers no element of personal insight. Negative humor stems from the desire to be superior to others.) Positive humor is delighting in the silliness of everyday situations and catching yourself being just a little too serious about life.

We've all used humor to release tension and reduce stress. Laughter has emotional and physical healing power. Positive humor reduces anxiety and stimulates creativity. In counseling, I've often found that a good time to make a point is right after a good laugh, when

neither client nor counselor are taking the issue *or* the
counseling process very seriously.

When we're lighthearted, we don't misuse our
memories, block ego-conflicting information, distort the
world or limit ourselves via beliefs or insecurities. No
wonder laughing feels so good. It liberates us from the
quicksand of our own thinking.

Humor aids in making effective decisions and is a
natural by-product of self-understanding. It's difficult to
take ourselves seriously when we realize that we keep
distress alive *solely* in our own heads.

We Think, Therefore We Feel and Act

When we're angry at employees for violating
standards that reflect *our* self-images, *thought* is at
cause. When employees avoid responsibility for fear of
failing, their anxieties come from what they *think*. When
I'm stuck in a gloomy mood, it's because I'm feeding it
with my *thoughts*. When I'm anxious about making
payroll, my fears stem from my *thoughts* about failing,
losing the business, facing employees and so on.

We often lose sight of the fact that our values, beliefs
and insecurities persist through the same mental process
that brought them into the world—our thinking. This is
why understanding the significance of feelings is so
important. Negative feelings make dark thoughts darker
and more compelling. Positive feelings give us the
wisdom to see how we create life experiences via
thought. They free us from the web our thoughts spin in

low moods.

One windy day I walked into the kitchen while my girlfriend was blow drying a cat she'd just washed. If you've ever had to blow dry a cat, you know what a frantic experience it can be. I didn't see what she was doing initially and began to shut the door. Suddenly, the wind blew it shut with a _bang!_

In very slow motion, my friend turned and looked at me scathingly. She was obviously upset by the door's loud noise and prepared to give me heck. In my mind I begin to get defensive, ready to counter her attack with an explanation about the wind and that it wasn't my fault.

Fortunately, however, something clicked within me. Instead of becoming defensive, I ignored my incipient thoughts and angry feelings, walked over to her, said I was sorry and kissed her on the neck. You could see the anger dissipate like smoke in a breeze.

When you feel a low mood forming and have the insight and courage to ignore your own mental rumblings, the negativity can't build and your low mood will evaporate. Had I not had the inkling that my own thoughts were beginning to make me defensive, I could not have stopped the argument before it escalated. There are times, of course, when my thoughts get the better of me. But, always, in the back of my mind is a voice that says, "Relax, Allan, you're thinking yourself into an unnecessary mess."

Sometimes I don't catch myself soon enough. For example, I recently had a gift wrapped at a shopping mall. On the way to the gift wrapping service I walked through a department store. It occurred to me that the store was as capable of wrapping my gift as the service. My mood was low for some reason. Although I knew the store wouldn't wrap gifts not purchased there, I decided to try anyway.

First, I asked to see the kinds of paper available. The counter person said she couldn't do that because they had no samples. In my snit, I took that as a personal affront and insisted on seeing pieces of gift wrapping paper. Although this upset her, she tore off a couple of pieces and showed them to me. Feeling somewhat self-righteous (my ego was activated), I chose a color and asked her to wrap my gift. She, of course, then asked me if I had bought it there. Feeling slightly indignant, I told her I hadn't, but since she wasn't busy I was sure she wouldn't mind wrapping it. She refused to wrap it, citing store policy as the reason. This got my goat and we began an adversarial exchange. She continued to refuse. Our egos were in a battle to the death.

Finally, I called for the manager, but it didn't help. She backed up her employee. I became scornful, said a few biting words and left. I walked as far as the mall center and realized that my activated ego and low mood had caused the entire conflict. I stopped, turned around and walked back to apologize.

I heard the gift wrapping staff talking about me in harsh tones as I approached the counter. I apologized sincerely, taking full responsibility for the commotion. The counter people immediately lightened up and apologized for not treating me well. We all felt better. When I left the store, I knew that the rest of the day would go well for me and for them.

It took courage to go back and apologize, courage arising from the understanding that _my_ ego had created the problem in the first place. This same self-understanding and courage allows a manager to admit he's wrong. When you see that your ego creates most management problems, you learn to pay less attention to it. Sometimes you apologize after the fact, sometimes you catch your ego as it is activating and sometimes you see clearly enough to avoid activating it in the first place. In any case, you learn to recognize and distrust it.

Keeping Your Distance

Our brains are wonderful instruments, able to process thousands of bits of information every second. However, depending exclusively on them to manage human relations is like trying to measure the beauty of a sunset with a ruler—no matter how hard you try, you can't do it. You miss the point. Solving human relations problems requires a fresh perspective and distance, not analysis.

We solve problems in the present, sometimes with the help of information from the past. Our ability to think in the present depends on how well we understand our own thought process. Neither the past nor the future exist; right now is the only time that's real. We can't intervene in the future. We can only intervene in the present by finding the illumination we want _now._ The way we find that understanding is by dropping the thoughts and feelings that hold us back.

Most management problems come from a lack of self-understanding rather than ineffective techniques. Understanding leads to the positive feeling we have when we're functioning well as human beings. It means that our thoughts are serving us rather than tripping us up and we're not caught in a maelstrom of negative emotions.

Understanding happens naturally when we put a little distance between our thoughts and the world they create. We don't have to think anything particular in order to benefit from this fact. Positive thinking to counteract negativity, for example, assumes that positive and negative thoughts have weight, *all by themselves.* They don't! Negative thoughts are a mirage, and you can short-circuit the cycle where thoughts lead to low moods, bad feelings and even darker thoughts by treating them as lightly as they deserve to be treated.

Once we grasp this concept, our ability to manage others increases geometrically. Putting even a small distance between us and our thoughts allows us to deal with other people's upsets more compassionately. We're less likely caught in the problems or feed them. Distance enables managers to listen to hostile employees and act without making situations worse by getting defensive or self-righteous.

With the clearer perspective that comes with distance from the details of our thoughts, we trust our thinking less when we are in low moods. We can make better decisions because we don't treat our negative feelings as infallible authorities. It's glorious to know we don't have to pay attention to ourselves when we're depressed, angry or bored. We know these feelings are just the by-products of our own temporary mental malfunctioning. When we begin to get anxious or angry, we're more able to be gentle with ourselves and others. We're less judgmental, reactive and defensive. We lighten up and find that negative feelings pass more quickly. Our reactions to circumstances are often born of insecurity rather than common sense. Emotions are powerful motivators and our actions come from the way we feel. Our anger towards the employee who errs, the anxiety in our chest when cash flow is low, and the nagging doubts that nibble at our well-being when business is down are all caused by insecurity. It's true that we have to deal with the errant employee, the lagging cash flow and slow business. However, knowing that our emotional reaction is thought-created and is *not* based on anything physically threatening gives us the perspective necessary to manage people and solve problems like these more effectively.

Firing an employee is difficult for most of us because we know how traumatic it can be. When we're insecure about the process, however, and don't understand that our anxiety is a function of insecurity, we're likely to overreact to employees' upsets, making the process more painful than it needs to be. We might even blame the employee for causing our discomfort, creating an angry confrontation that can escalate to a legal crisis.

Sometimes it's obvious how to solve problems in the world of details and complexity. Seeking solutions without understanding how we create our worlds through our thoughts, however, is like searching for clams in the desert because it's easier to shovel dry sand.

What Do I Trust if I Can't Trust My Own Beliefs?

There's a significant difference between the thought process at the core of self-image and the innate intelligence that fills our lives with inspiration and enthusiasm. This latter wisdom appears most often when we're relaxed and enjoying ourselves. When we're taking a hot shower, sitting on the beach, watching a Hawaiian sunset, skiing ten-inch powder on a bright winter day, fishing, building a model train or seeing our children walk for the first time, we're probably exercising this inborn faculty. But, wisdom isn't reserved for the high moments of life; it is available to us at every moment of every day.

Wisdom is innate. It manifests when, as a result of self-understanding, we stop relying on our limited beliefs and values. Sometimes, in our dreams, solutions to problems arise out of nowhere. When we drop a subject, take a break or admit that we're stymied, we set aside our egos and free our minds to see fresh solutions. The process feels effortless and natural. Brainstorming works by releasing this innate knowledge. It's creative and fun.

Wisdom is actually beliefless. When you rely on it to guide decision-making and problem-solving, you're not using preconceived notions to find answers. You suspend judgments and expectations and, as a result, open yourself to new information.

The mental process that accompanies high spirits is warm, creative and effortless. It's a process that enhances your life and your business. As your self-understanding increases, your reliance on and ability to tap this source of natural wisdom deepens. It leads you and your employees to higher and higher levels of performance with less effort. In Chapter 1, Linda used this process to solve her perplexing and difficult situations with her salesman, John.

Self-understanding, which I've defined as appreciating how certain facts about our mental functioning (like the role of self-images, negativity and memories) affect us, leads to a greater use of innate human wisdom.

Why don't we use our innate wisdom more often? We're insecure because our egos are under attack. We're confused because we're relying on our limited knowledge to try to solve problems that call for wisdom, not analysis. We're burned out because we've trapped ourselves in a low state of mind and don't know the way out.

Many people are not used to depending on natural wisdom to solve problems. This intelligence and its power are often seen as a lucky fluke. However, tapping into your wisdom has nothing to do with luck; rather, it is _self-understanding that creates the state of mind that generates wisdom._

It's wisdom that opens the door to opportunities that others might call lucky breaks. Modeling this understanding—by being secure and in high spirits—is _a_ *fundamental managerial responsibility.*

It's uncommon for business leaders to use touchstones like states of mind to assess performance. Nevertheless, however, understanding where natural wisdom comes from and keeping it alive in an organization is the absolute answer to getting the most out of yourself and your employees.

Depending on morale as the source of high performance reflects a basic shift in attitude. It's comparable to seeing that the world is round after believing it's flat. This discovery simplified a mysterious phenomenon: ships disappear over the horizon because the world's round. Likewise, understanding the role of thought, ego, insecurity, memory and mood in human functioning simplifies the task of management. It explains the forces underlying employee motivation and gives managers a guide for setting policy.

Business leaders who recognize the importance of maintaining natural wisdom achieve remarkable levels of performance. Their businesses become the living manifestation of these leaders' high states of mind.

Different Realities

I've been a part-time career counselor and instructor for several years. Career counselors match people with jobs, a process that involves interpreting interest, values and aptitude tests. I've analyzed hundreds of these tests. It always amazes me how utterly different people are. Some people love clerical work, others door-to-door selling, and others physical exertion. A wonderful, nurturing setting for one is threatening and anxiety-provoking for another.

This brings me to an important fact: stress is in the eye of the beholder. I grew up in a cigarette-smoking family. To this day, whenever someone lights up a cigarette, I am suffused with nostalgia, not repulsion. I have the same reaction to diesel fumes because diesel motors were used to power ski lifts and the Rhine highway, where I took a marvelous motorcycle trip, is packed with diesel trucks.

A quiet, peaceful workplace is heaven for one person, boring for another. One person thrives on tight deadlines, another is paralyzed. Remember the hunters who didn't give a hoot about winning a trip to the ocean? This is a good example of assuming that what motivates me will motivate you. Put simply, each of us experiences a unique, thought-created reality.

When our egos are threatened, it's difficult to remember that others see the world very differently. With an increase in self-understanding, however, we can appreciate the differences in others and listen effectively. The ability to hear the viewpoints, judgments and ideas of other people depends on our state of mind. We can't hear anything new when we're defending ourselves.

I once worked for an agency that sponsored human relations training. We sometimes belittled each other's unique viewpoints. One day we realized this. We saw that when we planned even a simple car trip, one of us would worry about where we were going, one would worry about the cost, and one would worry about who was in the car.

Our disagreements ended as we saw that our conflicts had to do solely with differing belief systems—and the differences were worth enjoying.

If you take an honest look at the times you've become angry with an employee for doing something in a way different from *your* way, I guarantee you'll find a little piece of aggravated ego. As we distance ourselves from the self-righteousness of our egos, differences become interesting rather than threatening, a source of fascination and curiosity rather than irritation.

Just as brainstorming frees us from restrictions and judgments to come up with creative solutions, letting our employees be themselves opens the door to new opportunities and prosperity.

Seeing Is Knowing (Not Believing)

When I was 21, I spent a summer overseas doing missionary work. I met people who *knew* spiritual facts and people who *believed* them. Believers defended themselves, felt guilty about breaking rules, rationalized their actions, and thrust their beliefs on others.

The knowers, on the other hand, were confident, nonjudgmental, frank and practical. They had a sense of humor and accepted good and bad in others. They were serene in their knowledge and convictions. They taught by example. They used the same words as the believers, but the *depth* of their knowledge was dramatically different. Their knowledge was natural, a product of wisdom rather than wish or intellect. They were like the manager of the paint store who knew in his heart rather than believing in his mind that people deserve respect.

Each of the simple facts in this book can be believed through thought or known through insight. Belief is brittle; knowledge is durable. Belief is shallow; knowledge is deep. Belief can be complex; knowledge is simple. Belief can be negative; knowledge is always positive. Belief is something we struggle to make true; knowledge is always true. When we *believe* something, our egos depend on gaining converts, winning arguments and proving ourselves right and others wrong. When we know something, that's enough.

As we come to *know* through insights the role feelings, the past, ego and thought play in creating life experiences, our self-understanding grows. We realize that we can't change anyone but ourselves. We see that the changes that bring higher productivity come from within employees—they're not imposed upon them. Inspirational management depends on knowledge born of *insight,* not beliefs.

When I was young, I *knew* things about life I later forgot because they disappeared under hundreds of beliefs. In fact, I'm convinced that recovering what we already know about managing employees and relationships means remembering how it feels to be childlike.

Chapter 6

Recipe for Success

What characteristics do successful organizations share in common?

Businesspeople like to be problem solvers. They're inclined to confront human relations problems the same way they tackle production or financial problems—by focusing on the task and its outcome rather than the process.

They sometimes ignore emotional forces underlying behavior. "I don't care why you're always late. Don't do it again," or, "I don't care what you do on your lunch hour. When you're at work, don't make personal calls." This direct approach can be refreshing, given that excuses can sidetrack organizations. However, refusing to take feelings into account can be petty, and it reflects insecurity and bafflement about how feelings work to make organizations hum.

The other extreme, emphasizing an organization's emotional process at the expense of its financial well-being, is equally ineffective. It's a mistake to become obsessed by the reasons so-and-so is late every day, doesn't show up at all, underachieves or overachieves, isn't aggressive enough or is too aggressive, dislikes sales or production and on and on.

It is possible to strike a balance between these

extremes by understanding how thinking and feelings affect performance. What managers resist is the fact that permanent solutions for problems lie *first,* in their own understanding and *second,* in the specifics of the problems.

Sometimes the answers to problems are simple and straightforward. But even when the problem is a monster, the solution will work better in an atmosphere of loyalty, trust and respect. Solving problems in environments characterized by hostility, confusion and distrust is like pouring sand in the gas tank before driving. You may reach your destination, but I guarantee the trip will be hard and the engine will be a mess.

Each of our lives includes thousands of details. Every employee has different problems and different needs. They also have different histories and different ways of looking at the world. The number of specifics we deal with as owners, managers and supervisors is remarkable. When we keep our sights set on creating feelings of enthusiasm, respect and trust, however, we don't need to agonize over the specifics. *The details tend to sort themselves out.*

An example of this process comes from my interior designer friend, Bonnie.

One day, after returning from lunch, Bonnie met a co-worker who was complaining about the amount of work she had to do in too little time. Bonnie could tell that her colleague felt harried and needed to quiet down and feel better before all else. Bonnie physically dragged the harassed designer from the office to an outdoor cafe, where they talked over coffee. Within a few minutes of sitting in the sun and talking about concerns other than work, the designer's mood rose. She began to develop a perspective about her situation.

After an hour, they returned to the office. Because she was in a better mood, quiet and focused, the co-worker could organize her tasks and accomplish them efficiently. The following day she thanked Bonnie for helping her escape the hole she had dug for herself.

Time management problems seldom involve managing time. Rather, they're usually related to setting priorities and recognizing the importance of mood. People in high spirits manage their time well because they can see the big picture. People in low spirits have difficulty deciding what's important and what's not. They're trapped in the details.

That old saying, "If you want a job done, give it to a busy person," has a kernel of truth. The kernel is that busy people can often take on additional responsibility because they're directed. Activity arising from agitation or threatened ego, however, is frantic and unorganized. While doing human relations training, we noticed that people who were insecure and lacked direction frequently had very thick appointment books. This happened when their lives filled up with projects and events they could only remember by writing down. They didn't genuinely care about them and wanted to *appear* busy. The reason I remember this phenomenon is because I was one of these people. Those with thin datebooks, on the other hand, seemed to have a stronger sense of direction and clear priorities. They enjoyed what they were doing, knew what needed to be done, and knew when to do it. They were busy but could take on additional responsibilities because they had more space available in their datebooks (just kidding).

Sometimes it takes painful experiences to show us the futility of dealing with the world, our lives and our businesses in the same old ways. As our self-understanding increases, however, it takes less trauma to get our attention. As we become more sensitive to the power of positive feelings, we become less willing to put up with the internal and external factors that make our lives difficult. As we see how the past blocks positive feelings and high performance, we reject its negative pull. As we recognize the harmful effects of ego, we yield less to its influence.

There's an exceptionally busy medical practice in town run by a fine physician I'll call Dr. Jones. He enjoys his work and uses a gentle bedside manner, abundant compassion and wisdom in dealing with patients. Because Dr. Jones is human with human insecurities, however, he has blind spots. The understanding and wisdom he uses so successfully with patients breaks down when he manages his employees.

Although they're enthusiastic and dedicated, his employees feel considerable stress because the high patient load and unusual physical layout of the office create an unduly brisk pace. As a result, the staff is often sick. One employee left the medical field entirely, after a decade of experience in other offices, because she was so burned out.

Dr. Jones assumes that solving the burnout problem means hiring people who are comfortable working at a high pace. He believes that *employees* are to blame for their inability to handle so much activity. This assumption reflects Dr. Jones' failure to understand that a frenetic pace often leads to burnout *regardless* of who's doing the work.

People work naturally at different speeds but, whatever our inclination, mood affects our ability to handle fast pace. Frenetic, out-of-control activity can drown self-understanding, lowering our mood and limiting our ability to cope. Our good mood disappears when customers and phone calls overrun us and, as a result, we're less able to make decisions and manage information.

Dr. Jones doesn't recognize the effect of high pace on morale—or morale's input on performance. His office is caught in a cycle of sickness, burnout and turnover. With greater self-understanding Dr. Jones would intervene to address the morale problem. By working with his employees to improve their environment by reducing patient load, hiring more people or changing the physical layout—all motivated by a *sincere desire to be of service*—he would show esteem for his employees and enable them to do their jobs better. Dr. Jones' respect and trust would trickle down through his organization. Problems would solve themselves and the stress would subside.

The details of Dr. Jones' insecurities don't matter. His blindness might have to do with everything from money fears to people management anxieties. Rather than analyze the hows, whys, whos, whats and wheres, however, he needs to appreciate that anxious states of mind are the *cause* of his problems. He needs to sit down with his people and look for solutions.

Selected Positive Characteristics

All organizations are made up of people and their thoughts. In organizations that function at peak effectiveness, people exhibit a set of positive characteristics that include:

Loyalty—Faithfulness, being in service to a person, group, idea or cause, being supportive.

My father has an interesting saying he learned from *his* father. "He may be an *SOB* but he's *our SOB."* He valued loyalty highly and believed that one of the best ways to create it was to pay well and provide high quality perks. Still, I think even he would admit that compensation loses its potential to enforce loyalty after a while. A client of mine learned a lesson about loyalty. After giving a significant raise to one of his employees, the employee's performance dropped. This lackluster performer resented the company. He saw (correctly) that the raise was a manipulative attempt to make him work harder. He retaliated by working less.

Loyalty is, at its core, a positive feeling. Like all positive feelings, loyalty indicates that we're not polluting our thinking with our egos. Creating and maintaining employee loyalty in the long run depends on management's self-understanding, which dictates how employees are treated. We have to see how our *own* egos affect our state of mind before we can see how to influence employee performance. With self-understanding, actions are motivated by true esteem, not the desire to manipulate for profit.

It's possible to create the outward behavior of loyalty by punishing for disobedience and rewarding for obedience. *True loyalty,* however, is impossible to purchase. True loyalty is selfless; it comes from a sincere desire to *be of service* to a person, group or an organization. It is devotion without subservience. Self-interest has to be outguessed and manipulated. The desire to be of service is simple and self-rewarding. Acting in service to others feels much different than acting out of self-interest, and being in service results in sustained performance.

Good compensation plans help create an environment of security, but they don't guarantee loyalty and the desire to be of service. Ed (the manager of the paint store) knew how to create this desire. As a result, his employees paid less attention to job prestige (ego) and pay. The emotional benefits offset the low pay.

Certainly it's valuable to create motivational incentive/compensation programs (bonuses, profit-sharing, company dinners, etc.) that promote self-interest aligned with company goals. Unless a service environment exists too, however, organizations become stressful and eventually unfulfilling places to work.

It's wise to remember that people do what they do because of the feelings that follow. In a respectful, cooperative organizational climate, the feelings people want are easier to find because negative, ego-serving thought processes are not scuttling them.

Underneath all the hustle, bustle and power-seeking, people want positive feelings like enthusiasm, joy, satisfaction, trust, compassion and inspiration. Compare your business to your family. You wouldn't want to return home at night to a family that depended entirely on self-interest as the basis for spending time together. The carrots and sticks would be out of control—giant allowances and ridiculous curfews. A family life based on rewards and punishments would lack warmth and caring. On the other hand, family life based on mutual caring, respect and trust uses incentives as a natural extension of positive feelings.

When being in service is a belief rather than the result of self-understanding and a positive feeling, it no longer exists. When good qualities like compassion, tolerance and patience become part of our egos, they lose their *essence—good feelings.* For instance, creativity and the fear of looking dumb can't co-exist; neither can compassion and the fear of appearing weak. Accountability and resentment of management also cancel each other out. Creativity, compassion, clarity of thought and sense of purpose exist *naturally* when self-understanding is high. Clearly, self-understanding is the fountain from which all good things flow.

Creating an organization where employees are loyal to each other and to the company depends solely on managers' ability to feel in service themselves and to pass that on to their employees.

> Respect—To feel or show regard for, to prize or value highly another's opinion, wishes or judgment.

Feeling and showing respect for the judgments, thoughts or opinions of others is an outgrowth of being in service to co-workers. There are two kinds of respect: I can respect you for a specific attribute—your competence, for example. I can also *feel* respect, regardless of your skills and actions. Put another way, I can respect you for what you *do,* on one hand, or I can respect you for what you *are.* The latter comes from seeing you as someone like me trying to make sense of life, innocently stumbling over beliefs and subject to the same misuse of memory, self-image and thinking processes. Like me, *you are sitting on top of extraordinary potential.*

Respecting you for what you *do* is conditional—I respect you only as long as you continue to do what I respect you for. Respecting you for what you *are* is unconditional. It arises from self-understanding and focuses on your potential as well as what you accomplish. This kind of respect enables me to be forgiving and firm. I am forgiving because I understand why you're not living up to your potential. I'm firm because I'm less willing to put up with your game-playing and non-performance—I know you're capable of so much more. Respect arising from self-understanding enables me to work with you honestly and with an open mind because I'm not tied to my ego's idea of how you *should* act.

Respect begets respect. The negative plant manager I mentioned earlier respected very few people and got very little in return. The respect he felt was highly conditional; it depended on adherence to behavior just like his.

> Trust—Firm reliance in the honesty, dependability, strength or character of someone or something.

Developing trust, one of the key roles of management, starts with having the feeling ourselves. As with loyalty and respect, trust has as much to do with trusting our own knowledge as it does with trusting others.

We've come to associate trust with naïveté, but that's an invalid association. A person whose trust stems from self-understanding uses common sense to apply that trust in delegating effectively, tying the camel as needed. Trust, like love, is never blind unless it connects to our insecurities. I always work my hardest and try my best in organizations where I feel trusted.

> Cooperation—Working together toward a common purpose or end.

Teamwork is the natural outcome of feelings like mutual loyalty, respect, trust and enthusiasm. Setting up policies and procedures that reward cooperation is a good start, but trying to implement them without understanding that cooperation comes from positive feelings leads to a frantic and fruitless search for incentives that work. Striving for cooperation without self-understanding is an exhausting process of outguessing and manipulating employees.

Traditionally, team building involves using group process techniques to build the positive feeling of shared enthusiasm. As with all techniques, this works in a limited way, most often during a retreat or a few days with a consultant. As with most techniques, however, the results are not enduring. Cooperation fades with time. Employees who work together enthusiastically over the long run do so *naturally* in a positive work climate with wise, understanding leadership.

> Enthusiasm—Intense feeling for a subject or cause, inspiring, eagerness.

Enthusiasm is important in a business. Its presence signifies high productivity. It's one of the guiding lights of career counseling in that it is the active ingredient in job satisfaction and success. Find what you're enthusiastic about and you've found a career to love.

Enthusiasm is different from excitement, which combines enthusiasm with an element of fear. Managers sometimes make the mistake of promoting excitement rather than providing an opportunity for enthusiasm to grow in an organization.

Both excitement and enthusiasm are positive feelings.

Excitement, however, has a brittle quality to it. Excitement evaporates and needs constant reinforcement because it's partly ego-driven fear. And, because self-image is a part of excitement, it's possible to become addicted to it.

Enthusiasm is different. It comes from a deeper, quieter place within us where fear and anxiety don't exist. When we use the skills we love, for example, our enthusiasm is high and our burnout rate is low. And "time flies when you're having fun" —when you're enthusiastic. I'm enthusiastic about writing. As a result, hours pass without my noticing when I'm working on my word processor.

> Motivation—A reason or desire that acts as a spur
> to action.

Motivation can stem from fear and ego or from enthusiasm, respect, trust and loyalty. The former is short-lived and comes with side effects like stress. The latter has no side effects, benefits everybody and leads to high performance. Dynamic, long-term motivation is the product of self-understanding, not a pumped-up ego.

> Accountability, responsibility—Answerable, having
> to account for one's actions, being a
> source or cause, having a duty or
> obligation.

Accountability and responsibility, the willingness to acknowledge and accept your role in creating outcomes, are by-products of self-understanding. They can't exist in an insecure environment. The only reason people aren't accountable or responsible is because they're afraid and their egos are threatened. It makes sense to provide a reasonable amount of security in the form of wage guarantees, health benefits, pension plans and other kinds of programs designed to allay anxiety about the future. Just remember that techniques don't work in a blaming, stressful work environment.

Creativity—Inventiveness, imagination.

You and your employees are most creative when your self-understanding is strong and you're not serious, bored or anxious. When our brains are freed from the shackles of judgment, fear and doubt, as happens in brainstorming, they're virtual creativity machines.

Summary

The following flowchart shows how self-understanding leads to positive organizational characteristics:

Self-understanding

—perceiving the pitfalls of thinking and the role feelings play in our lives, appreciating our creative potential and innate wisdom.

⬇

leads to these feelings

patience	understanding
enthusiasm	a sense of purpose
courage	peace of mind
security	lightheartedness
compassion	satisfaction

⬇

which leads to these personal characteristics

clearer vision, mission and goals
better time management
clearer thinking
easier work life
easier, more satisfying relationships
more creativity
heightened need to serve others
higher productivity
more patience
less willingness to put up with negative games
better leadership skills
distrust of ego—in yourself and others

more flexibility
easier goal-setting
more respect and trust for others
more dispassionate
more accountability
better grasp of the big picture
better team-playing
heightened ability to delegate
better able to listen without judging
higher motivation
freedom from negative memories and thoughts
clear priorities
understanding
less stress, anxiety and burnout
detachment from mental and emotional turmoil
better able to manage with common sense

⬇

which, in turn, leads to these organizational changes

more teamwork and cooperation
better communications
easier problem solving
better customer relations
more consistent high performance and productivity
more adaptability
higher morale
less internal wheel-spinning
a clearer sense of mission and purpose
a less harried, anxious workplace
a more natural management style

greater loyalty
less conflict, stress and burnout
more fun
policies and procedures that reflect management's
     wisdom and desire to serve

Businesses can be profitable despite a lack of understanding. You and I can write the reports, meet the buyers, do the shopping, mow the lawn and wash our clothes in low moods. We won't do as well as we might otherwise, but we'll get by. However, businesses and people who profit despite low morale remind me of the old joke that the operation was a success but the patient died. Working with others and managing human relations shouldn't be a struggle. Managers who understand the source of feelings and the tie between feelings and behavior are well on their way to consistent success.

Chapter 7

Postscript

Leadership, vision and wisdom

Sometimes my own mood is low. Sometimes I'm anxious, doubtful, bored or depressed. When I'm upset, I write more carefully so my words won't reflect my lack of understanding. I also know that eventually my spirits will rise. Accepting my periodic low moods and writing cautiously while I feel this way is how I maintain this book's integrity; I recommend you manage your people the same way. When your moods are low, the yellow caution light is on, signaling you to go slow. Hurrying when you feel anxious or upset is like driving faster as the road gets rough and narrow.

I can't overemphasize the role of intangibles in the workplace. People in general and business people in particular are sometimes indifferent to the importance of feelings, thought and ego. Part of that ambivalence— even hostility—is due to the traditional emphasis on the bottom line and measurable results. We've learned to believe that unquantifiable things don't count when it comes to productivity.

What we forget is that productivity comes directly from a blend of our moment-to-moment world view and our actions. Our performance is always based on the intangibles of thoughts and feelings. Unfamiliar though it may be to depend on an abstraction like self-understanding, it is the heart of how we conduct business and lead others every minute of every day.

Corporate mission and goal statements work well when they reflect the aims of top managers who operate at high levels of positivity and self-understanding. What often goes wrong with mission statements is that managers get caught up in day-to-day battles and lose their way—they forget what powers their enterprise and where it came from in the first place. The loss of a corporate vision leaves executives struggling in a vacuum of feeling.

Organizations prosper when managers have insight-generated *wisdom* about their own mental functioning *combined* with a clear *vision.* Your business vision is what you want for yourselves, your employees, your customers and the world in your most positive, inspired dreams.

The visions I'm referring to here are always positive. They come to us when we're enthusiastic and hopeful about the future, secure and inspired. They always reflect a desire to be of service. Visions ensure top-to-bottom organizational integrity because, as management's driving force, they can't help filtering down from managers through employees to customers.

Clear visions lead to organizations with integrity and purpose. What follows are two management visions. The first is a manufacturing company owner's dream and the second is vision for my consulting practice:

1. "Build a company that enables customers, employees and me *to go beyond* our expectations for ourselves."
2. "Guide management toward leading by *wisdom, vision, hope, simplicity and humor.*"

Notice that it's impossible to tell what each business does from these statements. That's because visions show how owners *feel* about their businesses rather than what their companies *do*. In the same way that actions reflect feelings, corporate activities spring from our visions.

Your inspired dreams determine how your business develops. Your company vision reflects *your level of self-understanding revealed in your business dream*. It mirrors your highest aspirations and wisdom about life. It proclaims your most positive hopes about yourself, your employees and your customers.

If your vision comes from insecurity (about money, for example) or never rises above preoccupation with meeting goals and objectives (the *result* of vision), your company quickly comes up against its limitations. Companies without clear, positive visions drift with the tides of the market and the moods of personnel. Unsupported by positive dreams, your dealings with employees and customers are uncertain and hesitant.

A clear, heartfelt vision enables you to manage effectively. It helps you deal with daily problems and develop strategies, frees your creativity and opens the doors to inspiration. It comes from deeper levels of self-understanding and unfolds in positive ways that serve you, your employees, your customers and the world. It influences how you feel and treat others. It affects how your employees treat each other and your customers. And it shapes how your customers feel about your business.

Every company develops specific, measurable strategies, goals and objectives (profit targets, sales projections and productivity indicators, for example). The durability of these specifics depends on the depth and positivity of your dreams. Visions and dreams are themselves unmeasurable. However, in living them, they create positive feelings like enthusiasm, respect, trust and compassion that lead to successful goal-setting and implementation.

Your vision lies in the answers to questions like these—answers that reflect you at your best:

"When I started this company, what did I fantasize doing for the world, my customers, my employees and me?"

"How do I want my company to *serve* the world, my customers, my employees and me?"

"How do I want my company to *feel* to the world, my customers, my employees and me?"

There are companies out there that are powered by dreams born of insecurity. The result is greed, fear and addiction to power. Like the old joke about the operation being a success but the patient dying, what's the point? Positive visions are sustained by wisdom and self-understanding. We all lose our dreams occasionally, but self-understanding gives us the power to return to the positive feelings our visions create and, in turn, make our organizations prosper.

Maintaining inspired dreams depends on understanding how the mind undermines them through insecurity and negativity. If your visions aren't becoming fact, take an honest look at your level of self-understanding. You'll often find insecurities and ego muddling up either the vision itself or the process of bringing it to life.

Sandy, a former employee, recently told me how a resort she enjoyed had lost sight of its mission—customer orientation—over the last few years. The facility had long operated as a family business structured around functional areas, with customer service as the central focus. When the resort grew, however, the controller took over, dividing it into profit centers that were responsible for making money without regard for the whole organization. As a result, the quality of service dropped. For example, the resort had always opened early on weekends. One Saturday, Sandy arrived early, as he had for years. To his chagrin, part of the resort was closed. Upset by the unannounced change of policy, he approached an employee for help. The employee told him, "That's not my department."

The loss of a service orientation here influenced management's treatment of employees which, in turn, affected customer service. Although the resort continued to make money, it became a less pleasant place to work as it developed a reputation for treating employees as commodities. The owners of the resort, forgetting the importance of maintaining a service orientation, created a bureaucracy where employees became unwilling to take responsibility for being in service to their customers.

The key to long-term recovery for this resort—and for any flagging enterprise—lies in rediscovering the original dream. Maintaining the business vision on a day-to-day basis, however, depends *entirely* on the self-understanding of management.

Successful managers recognize that we're all trying to live our lives the best we can, given the information we get about ourselves and the world. When we feel bad and our self-images have us by the throat, our lives are serious and a struggle. However, when we notice the relationship between our feelings, thoughts and self-images, we gain a perspective that soothes us and opens us to new information and inspiration.

People aren't good or bad. It's more accurate to say we are off-track or on-track to different degrees. We've been taught that growing up is a matter of bringing ugly and uncivilized impulses under control. Certainly, some negative behaviors need stopping. Addictions, crimes, and physical and mental abuses are destructive and should be ended *now*. However, those negative behaviors are *always* the result of negative thought patterns, negative feelings and, ultimately, a lack of self-understanding. When we're caught up in the negative forces that create negative habits and behaviors in ourselves or others, we block our ability to see how to end them once and for all. We didn't create misery on purpose.

We are as unknowing as children about the misery we create. We're not aware of the destructive nature of our perceptions, feelings and actions when we're defending our self-images and wallowing in the past. Compassion comes from forgiving ourselves for not being what we believe we ought to be and are afraid we're not. Seeing our own innocence precedes seeing the innocence of others. Once we forgive ourselves, we lighten up when others don't meet our ego-created expectations. The result is quiet clarity of mind and the ability to lead.

Beneath negativity and lack of understanding in the workplace is potential beyond the limits of thoughts and beliefs. When we learn to have faith in our feelings as guides, it becomes more difficult to stray off-track. The common sense facts in this book are a compass that points us toward decisions and actions that make our lives, relationships and businesses more satisfying. A small change in direction can have profound effects in all aspects of our lives.

We're all looking for the same feelings. Sometimes we become confused. We believe that the feelings we want are excitement rather than enthusiasm, oblivion rather than joy and gratitude and a pumped-up ego rather than self-esteem. We mistakenly believe we want control rather than security, high activity rather than high productivity, and anxiety and stress rather than enthusiastic motivation.

When we're at our best—when we're not stumbling over our own insecurities, egos or misused memories— we *know* that oblivion, control, turmoil and stress are poor substitutes for their much richer counterparts.

Once we see we're all looking for *positive feelings,* it becomes more apparent how to create a work environment where those feelings are the norm. When we drop the sandbags of our negative thoughts and old memories, we rise. A work environment which doesn't add these sandbags via frenetic pace or insecurity is naturally productive.

It's possible to create an organization that brings out the best in everyone and that operates consistently at a high level of productivity. It all depends on the personal transformation of management. Organizations grow out of management's level of understanding and positive feelings.

The list of characteristics that make up successful leaders is endless. They manage their time well. They inspire confidence in the people under them. They focus on those they lead and general goals rather than details. They're future directed. They're enthusiastic and adaptable. They delegate in non-authoritarian ways and focus on solving problems rather than blaming. They encourage cooperative input and teamwork. They avoid extensive rules and set realistic goals. *Every one of these characteristics is the spontaneous, inevitable by-product of self-understanding and wisdom.*

Certain issues crop up over and over in business. Motivation, productivity, incentive programs, absenteeism—all managers face these issues at one time or another. Though the setting is different, we face the same issues in other parts of our lives, too. Although the details differ, the solutions are the same. The truths described in this book have universal applications. They apply to our work relationships, our marriages, childrearing, friendships and how we live every day. Understanding them contributes dramatically to our ability to enjoy life and solve problems of the heart and the marketplace.

Feelings play the same role in a workplace and a relationship. Seeing how our employees' self-images interfere with their ability to make decisions is the same as seeing how our own egos and self-images affect our relationships with our friends and children. Knowing how employee morale affects performance is the same as knowing how our own ability to do what needs to be done depends on our mood. Understanding the role of the past in holding our organization down requires the same insight as understanding how we impede our personal growth by wallowing in our history. The benefits that come from understanding these basic, common sense principles *start with ourselves and spread to our interaction with others.*

Self-understanding enables us to use our natural wisdom, see what is real, and deal with it head-on. This reminds me of a true story told by a seminar leader that goes like this:

One morning I got up, walked to the kitchen and saw I was out of orange juice. I pulled a can of frozen juice from the freezer. I mixed the juice, poured myself a big glass and took a swallow. Horrors! It was awful. I thought that it must be spoiled and that I should consider rushing to the hospital. Fortunately, I decided to check the expiration date on the can. Well, son of a gun—it wasn't orange juice at all, it was tangerine juice. Tangerine juice may look exactly like orange juice but doesn't taste like it at all. I tasted it again. Sure enough, it was good tangerine juice, not lousy orange juice. It wasn't awful, it was delicious. Once I saw the truth, my experience changed 180 degrees.

Learning to manage others with the basic truths presented here is like seeing that bad orange juice isn't really orange juice after all. Seeing ourselves with this new understanding transforms the way we see employees and our organization. It changes our perception of what we need to do to get the best out of ourselves and our people.

Compassion, creativity and respect for others come naturally when we're content and satisfied, knowing that the source of the feelings we want is in us. Serving customers well is the by-product of feeling secure and enthusiastic about our jobs. Treating nature with respect and living lightly in the environment is common sense when we feel joy and gratitude in our lives. And, finally, just as treating others with dignity and respect is natural when we're in a good mood, running a business with firmness, purpose and inspiration is the natural result of high morale.

I hope that you recognize a part of yourself in these pages, the part that has the wisdom, common sense and knowledge to manage others effectively, with patience, firmness and compassion. Welcome to a fantastic new adventure in working with others.

Recommended Resources

Flood, Allan.
    Audio recording –
        "Mind, Thought, Consciousness and Healing,"
        available for digital download for a nominal fee
        (contact Allan at **aflood@q.com**).
    Books –
        1) "Management by Inspiration" (2 editions), the
        most recent in 2020 (CCB Publishing),
        2) "Perfect Misfortune," (5 editions), the most
        recent in 2020 (CCB Publishing).
    Master's Degree Thesis –
        "Human Relations Trainers: An
        Ethnomethodological Exploration of Issues
        and Effects," 1980.

Allan is the Program Developer and Grant Writer for a Federally Qualified Health Center in Oregon. For information about how he could work with you or your organization contact him at: **aflood@q.com**

For information and to contact Allan Flood:

Facebook: **https://www.facebook.com/allan000000**

Facebook: **https://www.facebook.com/allan.flood.18**

E-mail: **aflood@q.com**

www.ingramcontent.com/pod-product-compliance
Lightning Source LLC
Chambersburg PA
CBHW031945190326
41519CB00007B/674